CW01550030

The Ultimate Ninja Dual Zone Air Fryer Cookbook for UK

2000 Days of Quick & Delightful 2-Basket Air Fryer Recipes, Perfect for Beginners to Master the Art of Effortless Cooking with the Innovative Ninja Dual Zone Air Fryer

Desimir Forthington

© **Copyright 2024 Desimir Forthington - All Rights Reserved.**

It is in no way legal to reproduce, duplicate, or transmit any part of this document by either electronic means or in printed format. Recording of this publication is strictly prohibited, and any storage of this material is not allowed unless with written permission from the publisher. All rights reserved.

The information provided herein is stated to be truthful and consistent, in that any liability, regarding inattention or otherwise, by any usage or abuse of any policies, processes, or directions contained within is the solitary and complete responsibility of the recipient reader. Under no circumstances will any legal liability or blame be held against the publisher for any reparation, damages, or monetary loss due to the information herein, either directly or indirectly.

Respective authors own all copyrights not held by the publisher.

Legal Notice:

This book is copyright protected. This is only for personal use. You cannot amend, distribute, sell, use, quote or paraphrase any part of the content within this book without the consent of the author or copyright owner. Legal action will be pursued if this is breached.

Disclaimer Notice:

Please note the information contained within this document is for educational and entertainment purposes only. Every attempt has been made to provide accurate, up-to-date, reliable, and complete information. No warranties of any kind are expressed or implied. Readers acknowledge that the author is not engaging in the rendering of legal, financial, medical or professional advice.

By reading this document, the reader agrees that under no circumstances are we responsible for any losses, direct or indirect, which are incurred as a result of the use of information contained within this document, including, but not limited to, errors, omissions, or inaccuracies.

Table of Contents

INTRODUCTION

Structural Compositions

The Ninja Foodi Dual Zone Air Fryer is a marvel of modern kitchen technology, combining functionality, efficiency, and convenience in a sleek and stylish package. To understand its structural composition, let's delve into its various components and how they work together to deliver exceptional cooking results.

Main Body: The main body of the air fryer houses the electronic controls, display panel, heating elements, and fan systems. It's where all the magic happens. The design is typically compact and space-efficient, allowing it to fit neatly on your countertop without taking up too much room.

Dual Cooking Zones: One of the standout features of this air fryer is its dual-zone design, which allows for independent cooking in two separate compartments. Each zone has its own cooking basket, heating element, and fan. This innovative design enables users to cook two different dishes simultaneously at different temperatures and cooking times, maximizing efficiency and versatility.

Cooking Baskets: The cooking baskets are where the food is placed for air frying. They are typically removable for easy loading and unloading of ingredients and feature a non-stick coating for effortless cleanup. The baskets are designed to maximize air circulation around the food, ensuring even cooking and crispy results every time.

Heating Elements: Located above and below each cooking basket, the heating elements generate the heat necessary for cooking. They are precision-engineered to deliver consistent and uniform heat distribution throughout the cooking chamber, ensuring that food is cooked thoroughly and evenly.

Fan Systems: The fan systems are responsible for circulating hot air around the cooking chamber at high speeds, creating the signature crispiness associated with air frying. They help to distribute heat evenly, prevent hot spots, and ensure that food cooks quickly and efficiently.

Control Panel: The control panel is where users can select cooking functions, adjust time and temperature settings, and monitor the progress of their cooking. It typically features an intuitive interface with easy-to-read displays and responsive touch controls for seamless operation.

Copper Accents: Adding a touch of elegance to the design, sleek copper accents adorn various parts of the air fryer, enhancing its aesthetic appeal and making it a stylish addition to any kitchen.

Accessories: Along with the air fryer itself, the package may include accessories such as silicone tongs for easy handling of food, additional cooking racks or trays, and a recipe book for inspiration and guidance.

In summary, the structural composition of the Ninja Foodi Dual Zone Air Fryer is a carefully engineered blend of innovative design, high-quality materials, and advanced technology. From its dual cooking zones to its precision heating elements and intuitive control panel, every component works together seamlessly to deliver delicious, crispy results with every use.

Functions and Benefits

The 6-in-1 Ninja Foodi Dual Zone Air Fryer is a versatile kitchen appliance that offers a range of functions and benefits to enhance your cooking experience. Let's delve into each of its functions and explore the advantages they bring to your culinary adventures:

- Max Crisp Function:

  The Max Crisp function is designed to deliver maximum crispiness to your food, ensuring a satisfying crunch without the need for excess oil.

  Benefit: Enjoy guilt-free indulgence with crispy favorites like French fries,

chicken wings, or onion rings, all with significantly reduced oil content compared to traditional frying methods. It's perfect for those who crave crunchy textures without compromising on health.

- Air Fry Function:

The Air Fry function utilizes rapid air circulation to cook food evenly and efficiently, resulting in crispy exteriors and tender interiors.

Benefit: With up to 75% less fat than deep frying, this function allows you to enjoy fried favorites with significantly fewer calories. From fried chicken to vegetables, air frying provides a healthier alternative to traditional frying methods without sacrificing taste or texture.

- Roast Function:

The Roast function evenly cooks meats and vegetables, sealing in juices for succulent results.

Benefit: Experience perfectly roasted meats with tender, juicy interiors and caramelized exteriors. Whether you're roasting a whole chicken, a rack of lamb, or a medley of vegetables, this function ensures consistent and delicious results every time.

- Bake Function:

The Bake function offers precise temperature control for baking a variety of sweet and savory treats.

Benefit: From cakes and cookies to casseroles and pizzas, the Bake function allows you to unleash your inner baker with confidence. Enjoy evenly baked goods with golden brown crusts and moist centers, all without the hassle of preheating a conventional oven.

- Reheat Function:

The Reheat function gently warms leftovers or precooked meals without overcooking or drying them out.

Benefit: Say goodbye to soggy leftovers and hello to reheated meals that taste just as fresh as the day they were made. Whether you're reheating last night's pizza or reviving yesterday's roast, this function ensures evenly heated results every time.

- Dehydrate Function:

The Dehydrate function removes moisture from fruits, vegetables, meats, and herbs to create homemade snacks and preserves.

Benefit: Preserve seasonal produce, make your own jerky, or create flavorful dried herbs with ease. The Dehydrate function offers a convenient way to enjoy healthy, preservative-free snacks that can be enjoyed on the go or incorporated into your favorite recipes.

In addition to its multifunctionality, the Ninja Foodi Dual Zone Air Fryer boasts several other benefits that make it a must-have kitchen appliance:

Energy-Saving: With the ability to save up to 65% on your energy bill compared to conventional ovens, this air fryer is not only convenient but also environmentally friendly and cost-effective.

Independent Cooking Zones: The dual-zone design allows you to cook two different foods simultaneously, each with its own cooking settings. This feature saves time and eliminates the need for multiple appliances, making meal preparation more efficient.

Extra-Large Capacity: With the ability to cook up to 8 portions at once, this air fryer is ideal for feeding a crowd or preparing meals in advance. Whether

you're hosting a dinner party or meal prepping for the week ahead, its generous capacity ensures you'll have plenty of food to go around.

Quick Cooking Times: Cook up to 75% faster than traditional fan ovens, thanks to the air fryer's rapid cooking technology. Spend less time waiting for your meals to cook and more time enjoying them with family and friends.

Overall, the 6-in-1 Ninja Foodi Dual Zone Air Fryer offers a multitude of functions and benefits that cater to a wide range of cooking needs. From healthier frying options to convenient meal preparation, this versatile appliance is sure to become a staple in any kitchen.

Tips and Tricks for Air Frying Success

Air frying has taken the culinary world by storm, offering a healthier alternative to traditional frying methods without sacrificing flavor or texture. With the Ninja Foodi Dual Zone Air Fryer, achieving air frying success is easier than ever. Here are some tips and tricks to help you master the art of air frying:

- Preheat Properly:

  Preheating your air fryer is essential for achieving optimal results. Just like with conventional ovens, preheating ensures that your food cooks evenly and consistently. For best results, preheat your Ninja Foodi Dual Zone Air Fryer according to the recipe's instructions. This step ensures that the air fryer is at the right temperature before you begin cooking, resulting in perfectly crispy and delicious meals every time.

- Use the Right Amount of Oil:

  One of the key benefits of air frying is that it requires significantly less oil than traditional frying methods. However, using too little or too much oil can affect the taste and texture of your food. To achieve the perfect balance, lightly coat your ingredients with a thin layer of oil using a spray bottle or brush. This helps to promote browning and crispiness without excess oiliness.

- Arrange Food Evenly:

  Properly arranging your food in the air fryer basket ensures even cooking and browning. Avoid overcrowding the basket, as this can prevent air from circulating properly and result in unevenly cooked food. Instead, arrange your ingredients in a single layer, leaving some space between each piece to allow for proper airflow. If cooking multiple items simultaneously, consider using the dual-zone feature of the Ninja Foodi Dual Zone Air Fryer to cook different foods at the same time without flavor transfer.

- Shake or Flip Halfway Through Cooking:

  To ensure that your food cooks evenly on all sides, shake or flip it halfway through the cooking process. This helps to promote even browning and crispiness, especially for foods like french fries or chicken wings. Use silicone tongs, included with the Ninja Foodi Dual Zone Air Fryer, to gently toss or flip your food halfway through cooking. This simple step can make a big difference in the final texture and flavor of your air-fried creations.

- Experiment with Seasonings and Marinades:

  Air frying is incredibly versatile, allowing you to create a wide range of delicious dishes with minimal effort. Experiment with different seasonings, herbs, and spices to customize the flavor of your favorite foods. You can also marinate proteins like chicken or tofu before air frying to infuse them with even more flavor. Don't be afraid to get creative and try out new combinations to discover your perfect air-fried masterpiece.

- Monitor Cooking Time and Temperature:

  While air frying is generally faster than conventional cooking methods, it's essential to monitor your food closely to prevent overcooking or burning. Keep an eye on the cooking time and temperature specified in your recipe, adjusting as needed based on your air fryer's performance and the size of your ingredients. The Ninja Foodi Dual Zone Air Fryer features customizable cooking settings, allowing you to tailor the cooking process to suit your preferences.

- Clean and Maintain Your Air Fryer Regularly:

  Proper maintenance is key to ensuring that your Ninja Foodi Dual Zone Air Fryer performs at its best for years to come. After each use, allow the air fryer to cool completely before cleaning it. Remove the baskets and trays

and wash them with warm, soapy water, or place them in the dishwasher for easy cleanup. Wipe down the interior and exterior of the air fryer with a damp cloth as needed to remove any grease or food residue. Regular cleaning helps to prevent buildup and maintain optimal performance.

By following these tips and tricks, you can unlock the full potential of your Ninja Foodi Dual Zone Air Fryer and enjoy delicious, crispy meals with ease. Whether you're air frying french fries, roasting vegetables, or reheating leftovers, mastering the art of air frying is sure to elevate your culinary skills and impress your family and friends.

Cleaning And Maintaining

Cleaning and maintaining your Ninja Foodi Dual Zone Air Fryer is essential to ensure its longevity and optimal performance. With its sleek design and multiple functions, keeping it clean not only extends its lifespan but also ensures that your food remains delicious and free from any contaminants. Here's a comprehensive guide on how to clean and maintain your air fryer:

- Regular Cleaning Routine:

  After each use, allow the air fryer to cool down completely before cleaning.

  Unplug the appliance and remove any accessories, such as the cooking baskets and silicone tongs.

  Wipe the exterior of the air fryer with a damp cloth to remove any grease or food residue. Be sure not to use abrasive cleaners that could damage the finish.

  For stubborn stains or grease buildup, you can use a mild dish soap solution and a soft sponge or cloth to gently scrub the surface.

  Dry all parts thoroughly before reassembling or storing the air fryer.

- Cleaning the Cooking Baskets:

  The cooking baskets are where most of the food residue accumulates. After each use, remove the baskets and empty any remaining food particles into the trash.

  Wash the baskets with warm, soapy water, using a non-abrasive sponge or brush to remove any stuck-on food.

Rinse the baskets thoroughly with clean water to remove any soap residue.

Allow the baskets to air dry completely before placing them back into the air fryer.

- Cleaning the Interior:

The interior of the air fryer may also accumulate grease and food residue over time. To clean it, use a damp cloth or sponge to wipe down the inside surfaces.

For tougher stains or baked-on residue, you can use a mixture of baking soda and water to create a paste. Apply the paste to the stains and let it sit for a few minutes before wiping it away with a damp cloth.

Avoid using harsh chemicals or abrasive cleaners inside the air fryer, as they may damage the non-stick coating.

- Cleaning the Heating Element:

Over time, the heating element of the air fryer may accumulate grease and food residue, which can affect its performance. It's essential to keep this area clean to prevent any issues.

Allow the air fryer to cool completely, then use a soft brush or cloth to gently remove any debris from the heating element.

Be careful not to damage the heating element while cleaning, as it is a crucial component of the air fryer's functionality.

- Maintenance Tips:

Regularly inspect the air fryer for any signs of wear or damage, such as frayed cords or loose parts. If you notice any issues, stop using the appliance immediately and contact the manufacturer for assistance.

Avoid using metal utensils or abrasive cleaning tools inside the air fryer, as they can scratch the non-stick coating and damage the appliance.

Store the air fryer in a cool, dry place when not in use, away from direct sunlight or heat sources.

Refer to the user manual for specific care instructions and recommendations from the manufacturer.

By following these cleaning and maintenance tips, you can keep your Ninja Foodi Dual Zone Air Fryer in top condition for years to come, ensuring that it continues to deliver delicious and healthy meals with every use.

Safety Precautions

Safety precautions are paramount when using any kitchen appliance, and the Ninja Foodi Dual Zone Air Fryer is no exception. While this appliance offers

convenience and versatility in cooking, it's essential to follow specific safety guidelines to ensure safe operation. Here are some crucial safety precautions to keep in mind when using the Ninja Foodi Dual Zone Air Fryer:

Read the Instruction Manual: Before using the Ninja Foodi Dual Zone Air Fryer, thoroughly read the instruction manual provided by the manufacturer. Familiarize yourself with the appliance's features, functions, and safety precautions outlined in the manual. Understanding how to operate the air fryer correctly is crucial for safe usage.

Proper Placement: Place the air fryer on a stable, flat surface to prevent it from tipping over during operation. Ensure there is enough clearance around the appliance to allow for proper ventilation and airflow. Avoid placing the air fryer near flammable materials or overhanging cabinets that could obstruct airflow or pose a fire hazard.

Preheat with Caution: When preheating the air fryer, be mindful of the hot air circulating inside the cooking chambers. Keep hands and other objects away from the air vents to prevent burns or injuries. Use the provided handles or knobs to operate the appliance safely.

Use Oven Mitts or Silicone Tongs: When handling hot trays or baskets from the air fryer, always use oven mitts or silicone tongs to protect your hands from burns. The cooking chambers can reach high temperatures during operation, so exercise caution when removing cooked food or adjusting trays.

Avoid Overfilling: Do not overfill the cooking chambers beyond the recommended capacity specified by the manufacturer. Overfilling can obstruct airflow and lead to uneven cooking results or potential damage to the appliance. Follow the recommended portion sizes and cooking instructions provided in the recipe book or user manual.

Monitor Cooking Progress: Keep an eye on your food while it's cooking in the air fryer. Avoid leaving the appliance unattended during operation to prevent accidental spills, overcooking, or other mishaps. Use the timer and temperature controls to regulate the cooking process effectively.

Keep Children and Pets Away: Always supervise children and pets around the Ninja Foodi Dual Zone Air Fryer, especially during operation. The appliance generates heat and hot air, which can cause burns if touched accidentally. Ensure that children and pets maintain a safe distance from the appliance to prevent injuries.

Clean Regularly: Proper maintenance and cleaning are essential for safe and efficient operation of the air fryer. Follow the cleaning instructions provided in the user manual to remove food residue, grease, and other debris from the cooking chambers, trays, and accessories. Ensure the appliance is unplugged and completely cooled before cleaning to prevent electrical hazards.

Use Recommended Accessories: Only use accessories and replacement parts recommended by the manufacturer for the Ninja Foodi Dual Zone Air Fryer. Using incompatible accessories or aftermarket parts may compromise the appliance's performance or safety features.

Unplug When Not in Use: When the air fryer is not in use, always unplug it from the power outlet to prevent accidental activation or electrical hazards. Allow the appliance to cool down completely before storing it away.

By following these safety precautions, you can enjoy using the Ninja Foodi Dual Zone Air Fryer with confidence, knowing that you're minimizing the risk of accidents or injuries during operation. Always prioritize safety when cooking with any kitchen appliance to protect yourself, your loved ones, and your home.

Chapter 1: Breakfast

Blueberry Lemon Ricotta Pancakes

Prep Time: 15 Minutes   Cook Time: 10 Minutes   Serves: 4

Ingredients:

- 1 1/2 cups all-purpose flour
- 2 tablespoons granulated sugar
- 2 teaspoons baking powder
- 1/2 teaspoon baking soda
- 1/2 teaspoon salt
- 1 cup ricotta cheese
- 1 cup milk
- 2 large eggs
- 1 tablespoon lemon zest
- 1 cup fresh blueberries
- Butter or oil for cooking
- Maple syrup for serving

Directions:

1. Preheat one basket to bake at 180°C for 5 minutes and choose the SYNC option.
2. In a large mixing bowl, whisk together the flour, sugar, baking powder, baking soda, and salt.
3. In another bowl, mix together the ricotta cheese, milk, eggs, and lemon zest until smooth.
4. Pour the wet ingredients into the dry ingredients and mix until just combined.
5. Gently fold in the fresh blueberries.
6. Once preheated, lightly grease the basket with butter or oil.
7. Pour 1/4 cup of pancake batter into each compartment of the basket, spreading it slightly with a spoon.
8. Bake for 8-10 minutes until the pancakes are golden brown and cooked through.
9. While the pancakes are baking, preheat the second basket to air fry at 200°C for 5 minutes.
10. Optionally, place cooked breakfast sausages or bacon in the second basket and air fry for 5-7 minutes until heated through.
11. Once the pancakes are done, remove them from the first basket.

Nutritional Value (Amount per Serving):

Calories: 535; Fat: 20.1; Carb: 74.33; Protein: 15.53

Crispy Bacon and Egg Muffins

Prep Time: 10 Minutes   Cook Time: 10 Minutes   Serves: 4

Ingredients:

- 4 English muffins, split
- 8 slices of back bacon
- 4 large eggs
- Salt and pepper to taste
- Butter for spreading

Directions:

1. Preheat the air fryer to Max Crisp at 200°C for 5 minutes and choose the MATCH option.
2. While preheating, toast the English muffins in a toaster.
3. Once preheated, place the bacon slices in the basket.
4. Max Crisp the bacon for 5-7 minutes until crispy.
5. While the bacon is cooking, crack one egg into each compartment of the second basket.
6. Max Crisp the eggs for 4-5 minutes until cooked to desired doneness.
7. Once the bacon and eggs are done, remove them from the air fryer.
8. Spread butter on the toasted English muffins.
9. Assemble the muffins with bacon and a fried egg on each.
10. Season with salt and pepper to taste.
11. Serve the crispy bacon and egg muffins hot, accompanied by a side of grilled tomatoes or avocado slices if desired.

Nutritional Value (Amount per Serving):

Calories: 407; Fat: 27.16; Carb: 27.64; Protein: 14.4

French Toast Sticks

Prep Time: 10 Minutes   Cook Time: 10 Minutes   Serves: 4

Ingredients:

- 8 slices of bread
- 2 large eggs
- 1/4 cup milk
- 1 teaspoon vanilla extract
- 1 teaspoon ground cinnamon
- Maple syrup for serving

Directions:

1. Preheat the air fryer to Bake at 180°C for 5 minutes and choose the MATCH option.
2. While preheating, cut each slice of bread into 3 sticks.
3. In a shallow dish, whisk together the eggs, milk, vanilla extract, and ground cinnamon.
4. Dip each bread stick into the egg mixture, coating evenly.
5. Once preheated, place the coated bread sticks in the baskets.
6. Bake for 8-10 minutes until golden and crispy.
7. Once the French toast sticks are done, remove them from the air fryer.
8. Serve the French toast sticks hot, accompanied by maple syrup for dipping.

Nutritional Value (Amount per Serving):

Calories: 202; Fat: 4.11; Carb: 35.37; Protein: 5.4

Baked Beans on Toast

Prep Time: 5 Minutes   Cook Time: 10 Minutes   Serves: 4

Ingredients:

- 4 slices of bread
- 1 can (400g) baked beans
- Butter for spreading
- Salt and pepper to taste
- Optional toppings: grated cheese, chopped parsley, hot sauce

Directions:

1. Preheat the air fryer to Bake at 180°C for 5 minutes and choose the MATCH option.
2. While preheating, toast the slices of bread in a toaster.
3. Once preheated, spread butter on the toasted bread slices.
4. Divide the baked beans evenly among the bread slices.
5. Season with salt and pepper to taste.
6. Optionally, sprinkle grated cheese over the baked beans.
7. Place the topped bread slices in the baskets.
8. Bake for 5-7 minutes until the beans are heated through and the bread is crispy.
9. Once done, remove the baked beans on toast from the air fryer.
10. Garnish with chopped parsley and serve hot, optionally with a drizzle of hot sauce.

Nutritional Value (Amount per Serving):

Calories: 73; Fat: 2.13; Carb: 11.19; Protein: 2.48

Breakfast Sausage Rolls

Prep Time: 10 Minutes   Cook Time: 15 Minutes   Serves: 4

Ingredients:

- 1 sheet of ready-rolled puff pastry
- 8 breakfast sausages
- 1 egg, beaten (for egg wash)
- Tomato ketchup or brown sauce for serving

Directions:

1. Preheat the air fryer to Bake at 180°C for 5 minutes and choose the MATCH option.
2. While preheating, cut the puff pastry sheet into 4 equal squares.
3. Place 2 breakfast sausages diagonally across each square of pastry.

4. Roll the pastry around the sausages to form rolls, sealing the edges with a little beaten egg.
5. Brush the tops of the sausage rolls with beaten egg for a golden finish.
6. Once preheated, place the sausage rolls in the baskets.
7. Bake for 12-15 minutes until the pastry is golden brown and cooked through.
8. Once done, remove the sausage rolls from the air fryer.
9. Serve the breakfast sausage rolls hot, accompanied by tomato ketchup or brown sauce for dipping.

Nutritional Value (Amount per Serving):

Calories: 925; Fat: 66.15; Carb: 53.54; Protein: 28.09

Breakfast Banana Split

Prep Time: 10 Minutes   Cook Time: 5 Minutes   Serves: 4

Ingredients:

- 2 large bananas, peeled and halved lengthwise
- 4 tablespoons Greek yogurt
- 4 tablespoons granola
- 2 tablespoons honey
- 2 tablespoons chopped nuts (e.g., almonds, walnuts, or pecans)
- Fresh berries for garnish (e.g., strawberries, blueberries, raspberries)

Directions:

1. Preheat the air fryer to Dehydrate at 70°C for 5 minutes and choose the MATCH option.
2. While preheating, place the halved bananas in the basket.
3. Dehydrate the bananas for 3-4 minutes until slightly softened and caramelized.
4. Once done, remove the bananas from the air fryer.
5. Assemble the breakfast banana splits by placing two banana halves in each serving dish.
6. Top each banana with a dollop of Greek yogurt.
7. Sprinkle granola over the yogurt.
8. Drizzle honey over the granola.
9. Sprinkle chopped nuts over the honey.
10. Garnish with fresh berries.
11. Serve the breakfast banana splits immediately, offering spoons for scooping.

Nutritional Value (Amount per Serving):

Calories: 209; Fat: 7.07; Carb: 33.3; Protein: 5.96

Crispy Potato Hash Browns

Prep Time: 15 Minutes   Cook Time: 20 Minutes   Serves: 4

Ingredients:

- 4 medium potatoes, peeled and grated
- 1 small onion, finely chopped
- 2 tablespoons all-purpose flour
- Salt and pepper to taste
- Cooking spray

Directions:

1. Preheat the air fryer to Max Crisp at 200°C for 5 minutes and choose the MATCH option.
2. While preheating, squeeze excess moisture from the grated potatoes using a kitchen towel.
3. In a bowl, mix the grated potatoes with the finely chopped onion, flour, salt, and pepper until well combined.
4. Once preheated, spray the baskets with cooking spray.
5. Form the potato mixture into patties and place them in the baskets.
6. Max Crisp the hash browns for 15-20 minutes, flipping halfway through, until golden and crispy.
7. Once done, remove the hash browns from the air fryer.
8. Serve the crispy potato hash browns hot, accompanied by ketchup or your favorite dipping sauce.

Nutritional Value (Amount per Serving):

Calories: 209; Fat: 7.07; Carb: 33.3; Protein: 5.96

Air Fryer Breakfast Pastries

Prep Time: 10 Minutes   Cook Time: 8 Minutes   Serves: 4

Ingredients:

- 1 sheet of puff pastry, thawed
- 4 tablespoons fruit preserves (e.g., raspberry, apricot)
- 1 egg, beaten (for egg wash)
- Icing sugar for dusting (optional)

Directions:

1. Preheat the air fryer to Air Fry at 180°C for 5 minutes and choose the MATCH option.
2. While preheating, cut the puff pastry sheet into 4 equal squares.
3. Place a tablespoon of fruit preserves in the center of each pastry square.
4. Fold the pastry over to create a triangle, sealing the edges with a fork.
5. Brush the top of each pastry with beaten egg for a golden finish.

6. Once preheated, place the pastries in the baskets.
7. Air fry for 6-8 minutes until the pastries are puffed and golden brown.
8. Once done, remove the pastries from the air fryer.
9. Optional: Dust with icing sugar before serving.
10. Serve the air fryer breakfast pastries warm, accompanied by a cup of coffee or tea.

Nutritional Value (Amount per Serving):

Calories: 699; Fat: 45.63; Carb: 62.22; Protein: 10.65

Roasted Vegetable Breakfast Skillet

Prep Time: 15 Minutes   Cook Time: 20 Minutes   Serves: 4

Ingredients:

- 2 large potatoes, peeled and diced
- 1 red bell pepper, diced
- 1 green bell pepper, diced
- 1 small onion, diced
- 2 cloves garlic, minced
- 2 tablespoons olive oil
- 1 teaspoon dried thyme
- Salt and pepper to taste
- 4 large eggs

Directions:

1. Preheat the air fryer to Roast at 200°C for 5 minutes and choose the MATCH option.
2. While preheating, toss the diced potatoes, bell peppers, onion, and minced garlic with olive oil, dried thyme, salt, and pepper in a bowl.
3. Once preheated, spread the seasoned vegetables evenly in the baskets.
4. Roast for 15-20 minutes until the vegetables are tender and golden brown, stirring halfway through.
5. Once the vegetables are roasted, create wells in the mixture and crack an egg into each well.
6. Roast for an additional 5-7 minutes until the egg whites are set but the yolks are still runny.
7. Once done, remove the skillet from the air fryer.
8. Serve the roasted vegetable breakfast skillet hot, with crusty bread or toast for dipping.

Nutritional Value (Amount per Serving):

Calories: 279; Fat: 11.52; Carb: 38.21; Protein: 7.4

Baked Breakfast Tomatoes

Prep Time: 5 Minutes   Cook Time: 15 Minutes   Serves: 4

Ingredients:

- 4 large beefsteak tomatoes
- 4 large eggs
- Salt and pepper to taste
- Fresh herbs for garnish (e.g., parsley, chives)
- Grated cheese (optional)

Directions:

1. Preheat the air fryer to Bake at 180°C for 5 minutes and choose the MATCH option.
2. While preheating, slice off the tops of the tomatoes and hollow out the centers.
3. Place the hollowed-out tomatoes in the baskets.
4. Crack one egg into each tomato.
5. Season with salt and pepper to taste.
6. Once preheated, place the baskets in the air fryer and bake for 12-15 minutes until the eggs are set.
7. Once done, remove the baked breakfast tomatoes from the air fryer.
8. Garnish with fresh herbs and grated cheese if desired.
9. Serve the baked breakfast tomatoes hot, accompanied by toast or crusty bread.

Nutritional Value (Amount per Serving):

Calories: 115; Fat: 6.46; Carb: 9.68; Protein: 5.92

Dehydrated Fruit and Yogurt Parfait

Prep Time: 10 Minutes   Cook Time: 4 Hours   Serves: 4

Ingredients:

- 2 cups mixed fresh fruit (e.g., strawberries, blueberries, raspberries)
- 2 cups Greek yogurt
- 1/4 cup granola
- Honey for drizzling (optional)

Directions:

1. Preheat the air fryer to Dehydrate at 70°C for 5 minutes and choose the MATCH option.
2. While preheating, prepare the mixed fresh fruit by washing and slicing as needed.
3. Once preheated, arrange the fruit slices in a single layer in the baskets.
4. Dehydrate the fruit for 4 hours until it is dried but still slightly chewy.
5. Once the fruit is dehydrated, remove it from the air fryer.

6. To assemble the parfaits, layer Greek yogurt, dehydrated fruit, and granola in serving glasses or bowls.
7. Drizzle honey over the top if desired.
8. Serve the dehydrated fruit and yogurt parfaits chilled, as a refreshing and nutritious breakfast option.

Nutritional Value (Amount per Serving):

Calories: 99; Fat: 2.48; Carb: 13.01; Protein: 6.46

Max Crisp English Breakfast

Prep Time: 10 Minutes   Cook Time: 20 Minutes   Serves: 4

Ingredients:

- 8 pork sausages
- 8 rashers of back bacon
- 4 large tomatoes, halved
- 4 large eggs
- 4 slices of black pudding (optional)
- 4 slices of bread, for toasting
- Butter for spreading
- Salt and pepper to taste
- Baked beans, to serve

Directions:

1. Preheat the air fryer to Max Crisp at 200°C for 5 minutes and choose the MATCH option.
2. While preheating, arrange the sausages, bacon, halved tomatoes, and black pudding slices (if using) in the baskets.
3. Once preheated, place the baskets in the air fryer and Max Crisp for 18-20 minutes until the sausages are cooked through and the bacon is crispy.
4. Once the meats are done, remove them from the air fryer.
5. Crack the eggs into the baskets.
6. Max Crisp the eggs for 5-6 minutes until the whites are set but the yolks are still runny.
7. While the eggs are cooking, toast the bread slices and spread with butter.
8. Once everything is cooked, assemble the full English breakfast on plates, including the sausages, bacon, tomatoes, black pudding, fried eggs, and toast.
9. Serve with a side of baked beans and enjoy a hearty start to the day.

Nutritional Value (Amount per Serving):

Calories: 418; Fat: 27.67; Carb: 30.87; Protein: 14.47

Air Fryer Breakfast Bagel Sandwich

Prep Time: 10 Minutes   Cook Time: 8 Minutes   Serves: 2

Ingredients:

- 2 bagels, sliced in half
- 4 slices of bacon
- 2 large eggs
- 2 slices of cheddar cheese
- Salt and pepper to taste
- Butter for spreading

Directions:

1. Preheat the air fryer to Air Fry at 180°C for 5 minutes and choose the MATCH option.
2. While preheating, cook the bacon in a skillet until crispy.
3. Once preheated, place the bacon slices in the baskets and Air Fry for 4-5 minutes until heated through.
4. While the bacon is cooking, toast the bagel halves in a toaster.
5. Crack the eggs into the baskets.
6. Air Fry the eggs for 3-4 minutes until cooked to desired doneness.
7. While the eggs are cooking, spread butter on the toasted bagel halves.
8. Once the bacon is done, remove it from the air fryer and set aside.
9. Once done, assemble the bagel sandwiches by placing a slice of cheese on the bottom half of each bagel.
10. Top with bacon and a cooked egg.
11. Season with salt and pepper to taste.
12. Place the top half of the bagel over the egg to form a sandwich.
13. Serve the air fryer breakfast bagel sandwiches hot, accompanied by a side of fresh fruit or salad.

Nutritional Value (Amount per Serving):

Calories: 760; Fat: 50.07; Carb: 51.68; Protein: 26.49

Roasted Mediterranean Veggie Frittata

Prep Time: 15 Minutes   Cook Time: 25 Minutes   Serves: 4

Ingredients:

- 6 large eggs
- 1/4 cup milk
- Salt and pepper to taste
- 1 tablespoon olive oil
- 1 small red onion, thinly sliced
- 1 red bell pepper, diced
- 1 yellow bell pepper, diced
- 1 zucchini, diced
- 1 cup cherry tomatoes, halved
- 1/2 cup crumbled feta cheese
- Fresh basil leaves for garnish (optional)

Directions:

1. Preheat the air fryer to Roast at 180°C for 5 minutes and choose the MATCH option.
2. While preheating, whisk together the eggs, milk, salt, and pepper in a bowl until well combined.
3. Once preheated, heat olive oil in a skillet over medium heat.
4. Add the sliced onion and diced bell peppers to the skillet and cook until softened.
5. Add the diced zucchini and halved cherry tomatoes to the skillet and cook for another 2-3 minutes until tender.
6. Once the vegetables are cooked, spread them evenly in the baskets.
7. Pour the egg mixture over the vegetables in the baskets.
8. Roast for 20-25 minutes until the frittata is set in the center and golden brown on top.
9. Once done, remove the frittata from the air fryer and sprinkle with crumbled feta cheese.
10. Garnish with fresh basil leaves if desired. Serve with crusty bread or a green salad.

Nutritional Value (Amount per Serving):

Calories: 252; Fat: 20.46; Carb: 6.02; Protein: 11.47

Baked Avocado Egg Cups

Prep Time: 10 Minutes   Cook Time: 15 Minutes   Serves: 4

Ingredients:

- 2 ripe avocados
- 4 large eggs
- Salt and pepper to taste
- Optional toppings: chopped chives, diced tomatoes, shredded cheese

Directions:

1. Preheat the air fryer to Bake at 180°C for 5 minutes and choose the MATCH option.
2. While preheating, slice the avocados in half and remove the pits.
3. Use a spoon to scoop out a bit of flesh from each avocado half to make room for the eggs.
4. Place the avocado halves in the baskets.
5. Crack one egg into each avocado half.
6. Season with salt and pepper to taste.
7. Once preheated, place the baskets in the air fryer and Bake for 12-15 minutes until the egg whites are set but the yolks are still runny.

8. Once done, remove the avocado egg cups from the air fryer.
9. Top with optional toppings such as chopped chives, diced tomatoes, or shredded cheese.
10. Serve the baked avocado egg cups hot, accompanied by toast or a side salad.

Nutritional Value (Amount per Serving):

Calories: 220; Fat: 19.27; Carb: 10.26; Protein: 4.94

Baked Breakfast Granola

Prep Time: 10 Minutes   Cook Time: 25 Minutes   Serves: 6

Ingredients:

- 2 cups rolled oats
- 1/2 cup chopped nuts (e.g., almonds, pecans, walnuts)
- 1/4 cup honey or maple syrup
- 2 tablespoons coconut oil, melted
- 1 teaspoon ground cinnamon
- 1/2 teaspoon vanilla extract
- 1/4 cup dried fruit (e.g., raisins, cranberries, chopped apricots)

Directions:

1. Preheat the air fryer to Bake at 160°C for 5 minutes and choose the MATCH option.
2. In a large bowl, combine the rolled oats, chopped nuts, honey or maple syrup, melted coconut oil, ground cinnamon, and vanilla extract. Mix well to ensure all the oats are coated.
3. Once preheated, spread the oat mixture evenly in the baskets.
4. Bake for 20-25 minutes, stirring halfway through, until the granola is golden brown and crispy.
5. Once the granola is done, remove it from the air fryer and let it cool slightly.
6. Stir in the dried fruit.
7. Transfer the granola to an airtight container once completely cooled.
8. Serve the baked breakfast granola with yogurt, milk, or as a topping for smoothie bowls.
9. Store any leftovers in an airtight container at room temperature for up to two weeks.

Nutritional Value (Amount per Serving):

Calories: 200; Fat: 11.1; Carb: 31.81; Protein: 6.46

Air-Fried Banana Pancakes

Prep Time: 15 Minutes   Cook Time: 10 Minutes   Serves: 4

Ingredients:

- 2 large ripe bananas, mashed
- 2 cups self-raising flour
- 1 1/2 cups milk
- 2 eggs
- 2 tablespoons sugar
- 1 teaspoon vanilla extract
- Butter or oil (for greasing)
- Maple syrup and fresh berries, for serving

Directions:

1. Preheat the Ninja Dual Zone Air Fryer to 180°C.
2. In a large bowl, combine the mashed bananas, self-raising flour, milk, eggs, sugar, and vanilla extract.
3. Stir until the batter is smooth and well combined.
4. Grease the air fryer baskets with butter or oil.
5. Choose Option 2 (MATCH) to cook all pancakes at the same time.
6. Pour the pancake batter into the baskets, filling them about halfway.
7. Air fry for 8-10 minutes, or until the pancakes are golden brown and cooked through.
8. Serve the air-fried banana pancakes hot, drizzled with maple syrup and topped with fresh berries for a delightful breakfast treat!

Nutritional Value (Amount per Serving):

Calories: 543; Fat: 15.72; Carb: 86.14; Protein: 14.59

Chapter 2: Chicken and Poultry

Chicken and Vegetable Skewers with Tzatziki Sauce

Prep Time: 20 Minutes   Cook Time: 15 Minutes   Serves: 4

Ingredients:

- 500g chicken breast, cut into cubes
- 2 bell peppers, cut intoa chunks
- 1 red onion, cut into chunks
- 1 zucchini, sliced
- 8-10 cherry tomatoes
- 2 tablespoons olive oil
- 2 teaspoons dried oregano
- 1 teaspoon garlic powder
- 1 cup Greek yogurt
- 1 cucumber, grated and squeezed to remove excess moisture
- 2 cloves garlic, minced
- 1 tablespoon lemon juice
- 1 tablespoon fresh dill, chopped
- Salt and pepper to taste

Directions:

1. Preheat the air fryer to Air Fry at 200°C for 5 minutes and choose the MATCH option.
2. In a large bowl, combine chicken cubes, bell peppers, red onion, zucchini, cherry tomatoes, olive oil, dried oregano, garlic powder, salt, and pepper. Toss until evenly coated.
3. Thread the marinated chicken and vegetables onto skewers.
4. Place the skewers in the preheated baskets, ensuring they are not overcrowded.
5. Air fry for 12-15 minutes, turning halfway through, until the chicken is cooked through and the vegetables are tender.
6. While the skewers cook, prepare the tzatziki sauce by combining Greek yogurt, grated cucumber, minced garlic, lemon juice, chopped dill, salt, and pepper in a bowl. Mix well.
7. Serve the chicken and vegetable skewers hot with tzatziki sauce on the side.

Nutritional Value (Amount per Serving):

Calories: 363; Fat: 19.04; Carb: 14.51; Protein: 33.93

BBQ Chicken Drumsticks

Prep Time: 10 Minutes   Cook Time: 25 Minutes   Serves: 4

Ingredients:

- 8 chicken drumsticks
- 1 cup BBQ sauce
- 2 tablespoons olive oil
- 1 teaspoon smoked paprika
- Salt and pepper to taste
- Chopped fresh parsley, for garnish (optional)

Directions:

1. Preheat the air fryer to Bake at 180°C for 5 minutes and choose the MATCH

option.

2. In a bowl, mix together BBQ sauce, olive oil, smoked paprika, salt, and pepper.
3. Add chicken drumsticks to the bowl and toss until well coated with the BBQ marinade.
4. Place the marinated chicken drumsticks in the preheated baskets.
5. Bake for 20-25 minutes, flipping halfway through, until the chicken is cooked through and the skin is crispy.
6. Once done, remove from the baskets and let rest for a few minutes.
7. Garnish with chopped fresh parsley, if desired, before serving.

Nutritional Value (Amount per Serving):

Calories: 509; Fat: 31; Carb: 6.98; Protein: 48.76

Crispy Chicken Wings with Buffalo Sauce

Prep Time: 15 Minutes   Cook Time: 25 Minutes   Serves: 4

Ingredients:

- 1 kg chicken wings
- 2 tablespoons olive oil
- 1 teaspoon garlic powder
- 1 teaspoon onion powder
- 1 teaspoon paprika
- Salt and pepper to taste
- ½ cup hot sauce (such as Frank's RedHot)
- ¼ cup unsalted butter, melted
- 1 tablespoon honey
- 1 teaspoon Worcestershire sauce
- ½ teaspoon garlic powder
- Salt to taste

Directions:

1. Preheat the air fryer to Max Crisp at 200°C for 5 minutes and choose the MATCH option.
2. In a large bowl, toss the chicken wings with olive oil, garlic powder, onion powder, paprika, salt, and pepper until evenly coated.
3. Arrange the seasoned chicken wings in a single layer in the preheated baskets, making sure they are not overcrowded.
4. Max Crisp for 20-25 minutes, flipping halfway through, until the wings are golden brown and crispy.
5. While the wings cook, prepare the Buffalo sauce by combining hot sauce, melted butter, honey, Worcestershire sauce, garlic powder, and salt in a

saucepan over medium heat. Stir until well combined and heated through.

6. Once the wings are done, transfer them to a large bowl and pour the Buffalo sauce over them. Toss until the wings are evenly coated.

7. Serve hot with celery sticks and ranch or blue cheese dressing on the side for dipping.

Nutritional Value (Amount per Serving):

Calories: 689; Fat: 46.36; Carb: 16.16; Protein: 50.36

Chicken and Mushroom Pie

Prep Time: 20 Minutes   Cook Time: 35 Minutes   Serves: 4

Ingredients:

- 500g boneless, skinless chicken thighs, diced
- 200g mushrooms, sliced
- 1 onion, finely chopped
- 2 cloves garlic, minced
- 2 tablespoons butter
- 2 tablespoons all-purpose flour
- 250ml chicken stock
- 125ml double cream
- 1 teaspoon dried thyme
- Salt and pepper to taste
- 1 sheet ready-rolled puff pastry, thawed
- 1 egg, beaten (for egg wash)

Directions:

1. Preheat the air fryer to Bake at 180°C for 5 minutes and choose the MATCH option.
2. In a skillet, melt butter over medium heat. Add diced chicken thighs and cook until browned on all sides. Remove the chicken from the skillet and set aside.
3. In the same skillet, add sliced mushrooms, chopped onion, and minced garlic. Cook until the vegetables are softened.
4. Stir in all-purpose flour and cook for 1-2 minutes to make a roux.
5. Gradually pour in chicken stock and double cream, stirring constantly until the sauce thickens.
6. Add cooked chicken back to the skillet. Season with dried thyme, salt, and pepper. Stir to combine.
7. Transfer the chicken and mushroom mixture to baking dishes that can fit in the air fryer baskets.
8. Roll out the puff pastry sheet to fit the top of the baking dish. Place it over

the filling, pressing the edges to seal.

9. Brush the pastry with beaten egg for a golden finish.

10. Bake in baskets for 30-35 minutes or until the pastry is puffed and brown.

Nutritional Value (Amount per Serving):

Calories: 912; Fat: 44.48; Carb: 97.82; Protein: 36.15

Garlic Parmesan Chicken Wings

Prep Time: 10 Minutes   Cook Time: 25 Minutes   Serves: 4

Ingredients:

- 1 kg chicken wings
- 2 tablespoons olive oil
- 3 cloves garlic, minced
- ½ cup grated Parmesan cheese
- 1 teaspoon dried oregano
- Salt and pepper to taste
- Chopped fresh parsley, for garnish

Directions:

1. Preheat the air fryer to Max Crisp at 200°C for 5 minutes and choose the MATCH option.
2. In a large bowl, toss the chicken wings with olive oil, minced garlic, grated Parmesan cheese, dried oregano, salt, and pepper until evenly coated.
3. Arrange the seasoned chicken wings in a single layer in the preheated baskets, making sure they are not overcrowded.
4. Max Crisp for 20-25 minutes, flipping halfway through, until the wings are golden brown and crispy.
5. Once done, remove from the basket and garnish with chopped fresh parsley before serving.

Nutritional Value (Amount per Serving):

Calories: 654; Fat: 4.07; Carb: 13.02; Protein: 53.56

Air Fryer Chicken Quesadillas

Prep Time: 10 Minutes   Cook Time: 15 Minutes   Serves: 4

Ingredients:

- 2 cooked chicken breasts, shredded
- 4 large flour tortillas
- 1 cup shredded cheddar cheese

- ½ cup diced tomatoes
- ¼ cup chopped fresh cilantro
- 1 teaspoon ground cumin
- 1 teaspoon chili powder
- Salt and pepper to taste
- Cooking spray
- Sour cream and salsa, for serving

Directions:

1. Preheat the air fryer to Air Fry at 180°C for 5 minutes and choose the MATCH option.
2. In a bowl, mix shredded chicken with diced tomatoes, chopped cilantro, ground cumin, chili powder, salt, and pepper.
3. Lay a tortilla flat and spread an even layer of the chicken mixture on one half of the tortilla.
4. Sprinkle shredded cheddar cheese over the chicken mixture.
5. Fold the tortilla in half to cover the filling, creating a half-moon shape.
6. Spray the top of the quesadilla with cooking spray.
7. Place the quesadilla in the preheated baskets and Air Fry for 6-8 minutes, flipping halfway through, until golden brown and crispy.
8. Repeat with the remaining ingredients to make more quesadillas.
9. Serve hot with sour cream and salsa for dipping.

Nutritional Value (Amount per Serving):

Calories: 402; Fat: 11.9; Carb: 33.29; Protein: 38.9

Roast Chicken with Root Vegetables

Prep Time: 15 Minutes   Cook Time: 1 Hour 30 Minutes   Serves: 4

Ingredients:

- 1 whole chicken (about 4 pounds), giblets removed
- 2 tablespoons olive oil
- 2 teaspoons dried rosemary
- 2 teaspoons dried thyme
- 1 teaspoon paprika
- 2 large carrots, peeled and cut into chunks
- 2 parsnips, peeled and cut into chunks
- 2 potatoes, peeled and cut into chunks
- Salt and pepper to taste
- Chopped fresh parsley, for garnish

Directions:

1. Preheat the air fryer to Roast at 180°C for 5 minutes and choose the

MATCH option.

2. Rinse the chicken under cold water and pat dry with paper towels. Place the chicken on a cutting board.
3. In a small bowl, mix together olive oil, dried rosemary, dried thyme, paprika, salt, and pepper to create a herb rub.
4. Rub the herb mixture evenly over the chicken, making sure to coat both the outside and inside cavity.
5. Place the seasoned chicken breast-side up in the preheated basket.
6. Surround the chicken with chunks of carrots, parsnips, and potatoes.
7. Roast for 1 hour 30 minutes, or until the chicken is cooked through and the vegetables are tender, basting occasionally with pan juices.
8. Once done, remove the chicken and vegetables from the baskets and let rest for 10 minutes before carving.
9. Serve hot, garnished with chopped fresh parsley.

Nutritional Value (Amount per Serving):

Calories: 1175; Fat: 39.08; Carb: 132.26; Protein: 78.53

Honey Mustard Chicken Thighs

Prep Time: 10 Minutes   Cook Time: 20 Minutes   Serves: 4

Ingredients:

- 8 chicken thighs, bone-in and skin-on
- ¼ cup honey
- 2 tablespoons Dijon mustard
- 1 tablespoon wholegrain mustard
- 2 cloves garlic, minced
- 1 tablespoon olive oil
- Salt and pepper to taste
- Chopped fresh parsley, for garnish

Directions:

1. Preheat the air fryer to Max Crisp at 200°C for 5 minutes and choose the MATCH option.
2. In a bowl, whisk together honey, Dijon mustard, wholegrain mustard, minced garlic, olive oil, salt, and pepper.
3. Place chicken thighs in a large resealable plastic bag and pour the honey mustard mixture over them. Seal the bag and massage to coat the chicken evenly.
4. Arrange the chicken thighs in the preheated baskets, skin-side down.
5. Max Crisp for 10 minutes, then flip the chicken thighs and Max Crisp for another 10 minutes, or until the skin is crispy and the chicken is cooked

through.

6. Once done, remove from the baskets and let rest for a few minutes before serving.
7. Garnish with chopped fresh parsley and serve hot.

Nutritional Value (Amount per Serving):

Calories: 966; Fat: 68.03; Carb: 21.62; Protein: 65.03

Lemon Herb Air Fryer Cornish Hens

Prep Time: 15 Minutes   Cook Time: 40 Minutes   Serves: 4

Ingredients:

- 2 Cornish hens
- 2 lemons, halved
- 4 cloves garlic, minced
- 2 tablespoons olive oil
- 1 teaspoon dried rosemary
- 1 teaspoon dried thyme
- Salt and pepper to taste
- Chopped fresh parsley, for garnish

Directions:

1. Preheat the air fryer to Roast at 180°C for 5 minutes and choose the MATCH option.
2. Rinse the Cornish hens under cold water and pat dry with paper towels. Place them on a cutting board.
3. Rub each Cornish hen with half a lemon, squeezing slightly to release the juice.
4. In a small bowl, mix together minced garlic, olive oil, dried rosemary, dried thyme, salt, and pepper to create a herb rub.
5. Rub the herb mixture evenly over each Cornish hen, ensuring they are well coated.
6. Once the baskets are preheated, place the seasoned Cornish hens breast-side up in the basket.
7. Roast for 35-40 minutes, or until the internal temperature reaches 75°C and the skin is golden brown and crispy.
8. Once done, remove from the baskets and let rest for a few minutes before serving.
9. Garnish with chopped fresh parsley and serve hot.

Nutritional Value (Amount per Serving):

Calories: 660; Fat: 23.63; Carb: 4.75; Protein: 101.16

Chicken and Vegetable Fajitas

Prep Time: 15 Minutes   Cook Time: 15 Minutes   Serves: 4

Ingredients:

- 500g chicken breast, sliced into strips
- 2 bell peppers, sliced
- 1 onion, sliced
- 2 tablespoons olive oil
- 1 tablespoon chili powder
- 1 teaspoon ground cumin
- 1 teaspoon smoked paprika
- Salt and pepper to taste
- 8 small flour tortillas
- Sour cream, guacamole, salsa, shredded cheese, for serving

Directions:

1. Preheat the air fryer to Air Fry at 200°C for 5 minutes and choose the MATCH option.
2. In a large bowl, toss chicken strips, sliced bell peppers, sliced onion, olive oil, chili powder, ground cumin, smoked paprika, salt, and pepper until well coated.
3. Place the seasoned chicken and vegetables in the preheated baskets, ensuring they are spread out in a single layer.
4. Air Fry for 12-15 minutes, stirring halfway through, until the chicken is cooked through and the vegetables are tender and slightly charred.
5. While the chicken and vegetables cook, warm the flour tortillas according to package instructions.
6. Serve the chicken and vegetable fajitas hot with warm tortillas and your choice of toppings, such as sour cream, guacamole, salsa, and shredded cheese.

Nutritional Value (Amount per Serving):

Calories: 583; Fat: 25.13; Carb: 53.55; Protein: 34.91

Teriyaki Chicken Skewers

Prep Time: 20 Minutes   Cook Time: 15 Minutes   Serves: 4

Ingredients:

- 500g chicken breast, cut into cubes
- 1 red bell pepper, cut into chunks
- 1 green bell pepper, cut into chunks
- 1 red onion, cut into chunks
- ½ cup soy sauce
- ¼ cup brown sugar
- 2 cloves garlic, minced

- 1 tablespoon grated ginger
- 2 tablespoons rice vinegar
- 1 tablespoon cornstarch
- 2 tablespoons water
- Sesame seeds and chopped green onions, for garnish

Directions:

1. Preheat the air fryer to Air Fry at 200°C for 5 minutes and choose the MATCH option.
2. Thread chicken cubes, red bell pepper chunks, green bell pepper chunks, and red onion chunks onto skewers.
3. In a small saucepan, combine soy sauce, brown sugar, minced garlic, grated ginger, and rice vinegar. Bring to a simmer over medium heat.
4. In a small bowl, mix cornstarch and water to create a slurry. Stir the slurry into the saucepan and cook until the sauce thickens, stirring constantly.
5. Brush teriyaki sauce onto the skewers, reserving some for later.
6. Place the skewers in the preheated baskets, ensuring they are not overcrowded.
7. Air Fry for 12-15 minutes, turning halfway through, until the chicken is cooked through and the vegetables are tender.
8. Serve hot, garnished with sesame seeds, chopped green onions, and extra teriyaki sauce on the side.

Nutritional Value (Amount per Serving):

Calories: 437; Fat: 21.77; Carb: 29.6; Protein: 30.68

Chicken and Spinach Stuffed Mushrooms

Prep Time: 20 Minutes   Cook Time: 20 Minutes   Serves: 4

Ingredients:

- 8 large mushrooms, stems removed
- 200g cooked chicken breast, shredded
- 100g fresh spinach, chopped
- 1 small onion, finely chopped
- 2 cloves garlic, minced
- 50g feta cheese, crumbled
- 50g grated Parmesan cheese
- 2 tablespoons olive oil
- Salt and pepper to taste

Directions:

1. Preheat the air fryer to Bake at 180°C for 5 minutes and choose the MATCH option.

2. In a skillet, heat olive oil over medium heat. Add chopped onion and minced garlic, cooking until softened.
3. Add chopped spinach to the skillet and cook until wilted.
4. In a bowl, combine cooked chicken breast, cooked spinach mixture, crumbled feta cheese, and grated Parmesan cheese. Season with salt and pepper to taste.
5. Stuff each mushroom cap with the chicken and spinach mixture.
6. Place stuffed mushrooms in the preheated baskets.
7. Bake for 15-20 minutes, or until the mushrooms are tender and the filling is heated through.
8. Serve hot as a delicious appetizer or light meal.

Nutritional Value (Amount per Serving):

Calories: 257; Fat: 14.98; Carb: 7.85; Protein: 23.49

Cajun Chicken and Sausage Jambalaya

Prep Time: 20 Minutes   Cook Time: 25 Minutes   Serves: 4

Ingredients:

- 2 chicken breasts, diced
- 200g smoked sausage, sliced
- 1 onion, finely chopped
- 1 green bell pepper, diced
- 1 red bell pepper, diced
- 2 stalks celery, diced
- 2 cloves garlic, minced
- 1 cup long-grain rice
- 400ml chicken broth
- 1 can (400g) diced tomatoes
- 2 teaspoons Cajun seasoning
- Salt and pepper to taste
- Chopped fresh parsley, for garnish

Directions:

1. Preheat the air fryer to Roast at 180°C for 5 minutes and choose the MATCH option.
2. In a large skillet, brown diced chicken breast and sliced smoked sausage over medium heat. Remove from the skillet and set aside.
3. In the same skillet, add chopped onion, diced green bell pepper, diced red bell pepper, diced celery, and minced garlic. Sauté until vegetables are softened.
4. Stir in long-grain rice and cook for 1-2 minutes.
5. Return the browned chicken and sausage to the skillet. Add chicken broth, diced tomatoes, Cajun seasoning, salt, and pepper. Stir to combine.
6. Transfer the mixture to the preheated baskets.
7. Roast for 20-25 minutes, stirring halfway through, until the rice is cooked through and the liquid is absorbed.
8. Garnish with chopped fresh parsley before serving.

Nutritional Value (Amount per Serving):

Calories: 600; Fat: 24.39; Carb: 50.98; Protein: 45.77

Piri Piri Chicken Drumsticks

Prep Time: 15 Minutes   Cook Time: 25 Minutes   Serves: 4

Ingredients:

- 8 chicken drumsticks
- 2 tablespoons olive oil
- 2 tablespoons lemon juice
- 2 cloves garlic, minced
- 1 tablespoon paprika
- 1 teaspoon dried oregano
- 1 teaspoon chili flakes (adjust to taste)
- Salt and pepper to taste
- Lemon wedges, for serving
- Chopped fresh parsley, for garnish

Directions:

1. Preheat the air fryer to Air Fry at 200°C for 5 minutes and choose the MATCH option.
2. In a bowl, mix together olive oil, lemon juice, minced garlic, paprika, dried oregano, chili flakes, salt, and pepper to create a marinade.
3. Add chicken drumsticks to the marinade and toss until well coated.
4. Place the drumsticks in the preheated baskets, ensuring they are not overcrowded.
5. Air Fry for 20-25 minutes, turning halfway through, until the chicken is cooked through and golden brown.
6. Once done, remove from the baskets and let rest for a few minutes before serving.
7. Garnish with chopped fresh parsley and serve hot with lemon wedges.

Nutritional Value (Amount per Serving):

Calories: 502; Fat: 31.19; Carb: 5.58; Protein: 48.2

Mediterranean Chicken with Roasted Vegetables

Prep Time: 15 Minutes   Cook Time: 30 Minutes   Serves: 4

Ingredients:

- 4 boneless, skinless chicken breasts
- 2 bell peppers (1 red, 1 yellow), sliced
- 1 red onion, sliced
- 1 courgette, sliced
- 1 small aubergine, sliced

- 2 tablespoons olive oil
- 2 teaspoons dried oregano
- 1 teaspoon dried basil
- 1 teaspoon garlic powder
- Salt and pepper to taste
- Lemon wedges, for serving

Directions:

1. Preheat the air fryer to Roast at 200°C for 5 minutes and choose the MATCH option.
2. In a large bowl, toss together sliced bell peppers, red onion, courgette, and aubergine with olive oil, dried oregano, dried basil, garlic powder, salt, and pepper until evenly coated.
3. Spread the seasoned vegetables evenly in the preheated baskets.
4. Roast for 15 minutes, stirring halfway through.
5. While the vegetables roast, season chicken breasts with salt and pepper.
6. After 15 minutes, push the roasted vegetables to one side of the baskets and add chicken breasts to the other side.
7. Roast for an additional 15 minutes or until the chicken is cooked through and the vegetables are tender.
8. Serve the Mediterranean chicken with roasted vegetables, accompanied by lemon wedges for squeezing over the top.

Nutritional Value (Amount per Serving):

Calories: 798; Fat: 46.73; Carb: 56.35; Protein: 38.83

Chapter 3: Beef, Pork and Lamb

Pork and Apple Casserole

Prep Time: 20 Minutes   Cook Time: 2 Hours   Serves: 4

Ingredients:

- 600g pork shoulder, diced
- Salt and pepper to taste
- 2 tablespoons olive oil
- 2 onions, chopped
- 2 carrots, sliced
- 2 celery stalks, sliced
- 2 cloves garlic, minced
- 2 tablespoons plain flour
- 400ml apple cider
- 400ml chicken stock
- 2 bay leaves
- 2 sprigs fresh thyme
- 2 apples, peeled, cored, and sliced
- Fresh parsley, chopped, for garnish

Directions:

1. Preheat Air Fryer to Bake at 180°C for 5 minutes and choose the MATCH option.
2. Season the diced pork shoulder with salt and pepper.
3. Heat olive oil in a skillet over medium heat. Brown the pork in batches. Set aside.
4. In the same skillet, sauté onions, carrots, celery, and garlic until softened. Stir in plain flour and cook for 1-2 minutes.
5. Deglaze the skillet with apple cider, scraping up any browned bits.
6. Transfer the pork and vegetable mixture to ovenproof dishes suitable for the air fryer.
7. Pour in chicken stock, and add bay leaves and fresh thyme. Stir to combine.
8. Place the dishes in the preheated baskets.
9. Air fry for 1.5 to 2 hours until the pork is tender, checking periodically.
10. Once done, add sliced apples to the casserole and air fry for an additional 15-20 minutes until the apples are tender.
11. Serve with chopped fresh parsley.

Nutritional Value (Amount per Serving):

Calories: 709; Fat: 36.43; Carb: 35.95; Protein: 58.66

Pork Tenderloin with Apple Cider Glaze

Prep Time: 15 Minutes   Cook Time: 25 Minutes   Serves: 4

Ingredients:

- 2 pork tenderloins
- Salt and pepper to taste
- 4 tablespoons olive oil
- 2 cloves garlic, minced
- 240ml apple cider
- 2 tablespoons wholegrain mustard

- 2 tablespoons honey
- Apple slices
- 1 tablespoon apple cider vinegar
- Fresh thyme sprigs, for garnish

Directions:

1. Preheat one basket to Roast at 200°C for 5 minutes and choose the SYNC option.
2. Season the pork tenderloins with salt and pepper.
3. In a bowl, whisk together olive oil, minced garlic, apple cider, wholegrain mustard, honey, and apple cider vinegar to make the glaze.
4. Coat the pork tenderloins with half of the glaze and let marinate for at least 30 minutes.
5. Once the basket is preheated, place the pork tenderloins in a single layer.
6. Roast for 20-25 minutes, basting with the remaining glaze halfway through, until the pork is cooked through.
7. While the pork is cooking, preheat the second basket to Air Fry at 180°C for 5 minutes.
8. Air fry some apple slices for 3-4 minutes until caramelized.
9. Once the pork tenderloins are done, remove from the first basket and let rest for a few minutes.
10. Serve the pork tenderloin slices hot, garnished with caramelized apple slices and fresh thyme sprigs.

Nutritional Value (Amount per Serving):

Calories: 556; Fat: 22.17; Carb: 27.83; Protein: 60.54

Pork and Black Pudding Scotch Eggs

Prep Time: 30 Minutes   Cook Time: 15 Minutes   Serves: 4

Ingredients:

- 4 eggs
- 400g pork sausage meat
- 100g black pudding, crumbled
- 50g breadcrumbs
- Salt and pepper to taste
- 1 tablespoon vegetable oil
- Flour, for dusting
- 1 egg, beaten (for egg wash)
- Fresh parsley, chopped, for garnish

Directions:

1. Preheat one basket to Bake at 180°C for 5 minutes and choose the SYNC option.
2. Boil the eggs for 6 minutes, then transfer to cold water to cool. Peel and set

aside.

3. In a bowl, mix together pork sausage meat, crumbled black pudding, breadcrumbs, salt, and pepper.
4. Divide the mixture into 4 portions and flatten each portion into a thin patty.
5. Place a boiled egg in the center of each patty and wrap the meat mixture around the egg, ensuring it is completely covered.
6. Dust each wrapped egg with flour, then dip in beaten egg wash, and roll in breadcrumbs.
7. Once the basket is preheated, place the scotch eggs in a single layer.
8. Bake for 12-15 minutes until golden brown and cooked through.
9. While the scotch eggs are cooking, preheat the second basket to Air Fry at 180°C for 5 minutes.
10. Air fry some fresh parsley for 3-4 minutes until crispy.
11. Once the scotch eggs are done, remove from the first basket and let cool slightly.
12. Serve the pork and black pudding scotch eggs hot, garnished with crispy parsley.

Nutritional Value (Amount per Serving):

Calories: 575; Fat: 43; Carb: 15.45; Protein: 31.5

Lamb Moussaka

Prep Time: 30 Minutes   Cook Time: 1 Hour   Serves: 4

Ingredients:

- 500g lamb mince
- 1 onion, chopped
- 2 cloves garlic, minced
- 1 teaspoon ground cinnamon
- 1 teaspoon dried oregano
- 400g canned chopped tomatoes
- Salt and pepper to taste
- 2 large eggplants, sliced thinly
- Olive oil for brushing
- 50g butter
- 50g plain flour
- 500ml milk
- 50g grated Parmesan cheese
- Pinch of nutmeg

Directions:

1. Preheat one basket to Roast at 180°C for 5 minutes and choose the SYNC option.
2. In a pan, cook lamb mince until browned. Add chopped onion, minced garlic, ground cinnamon, and dried oregano. Cook until onions are soft.
3. Stir in canned chopped tomatoes and season with salt and pepper. Simmer for 15-20 minutes until the sauce thickens.
4. While the lamb is cooking, preheat the second basket to Max Crisp at

200°C for 5 minutes.

5. Brush eggplant slices with olive oil and place in the second basket. Max Crisp for 8-10 minutes until golden brown and tender. Set aside.

6. For the bechamel sauce, melt butter in a saucepan over medium heat. Stir in flour and cook for 1-2 minutes until golden.

7. Gradually whisk in milk until smooth. Cook, stirring constantly, until the sauce thickens.

8. Remove from heat and stir in grated Parmesan cheese. Season with salt, pepper, and nutmeg.

9. Once all components are ready, layer half of the lamb mixture in a baking dish. Arrange a layer of eggplant slices on top, then repeat with remaining lamb mixture and eggplant.

10. Pour the bechamel sauce over the top, spreading it evenly.

11. Bake in the first basket at Bake at 180°C for 30-35 minutes until golden brown and bubbling.

12. Serve the lamb moussaka hot, accompanied by a Greek salad.

Nutritional Value (Amount per Serving):

Calories: 716; Fat: 41.53; Carb: 44.63; Protein: 43.9

Lamb Kofta with Tzatziki Sauce

Prep Time: 30 Minutes   Cook Time: 15 Minutes   Serves: 4

Ingredients:

- 500g lamb mince
- 1 onion, grated
- 2 cloves garlic, minced
- 2 tablespoons fresh mint, chopped
- 2 tablespoons fresh parsley, chopped
- 1 teaspoon ground cumin
- 1 teaspoon ground coriander
- Olive oil for brushing
- 200g Greek yogurt
- 1/2 cucumber, grated and squeezed dry
- 1 clove garlic, minced
- 1 tablespoon fresh dill, chopped
- Juice of 1/2 lemon
- Salt and pepper to taste

Directions:

1. Preheat the air fryer to roast at 200°C for 5 minutes and choose the SYNC option.

2. In a bowl, mix together lamb mince, grated onion, minced garlic, chopped mint, chopped parsley, ground cumin, ground coriander, salt, and pepper until well combined.
3. Divide the mixture into equal portions and shape into elongated kofta.
4. Brush kofta with olive oil and place in the baskets in a single layer.
5. Roast for 12-15 minutes, turning halfway through, until cooked through and lightly charred.
6. For the tzatziki sauce, mix together Greek yogurt, grated cucumber, minced garlic, chopped dill, lemon juice, salt, and pepper in a bowl. Refrigerate until ready to serve.
7. Once the kofta is done, remove from the baskets and let cool slightly.
8. Air fry at 180°C some pita bread for 3-4 minutes until crispy.
9. Serve the lamb kofta hot, accompanied by tzatziki sauce and crispy pita bread.

Nutritional Value (Amount per Serving):

Calories: 554; Fat: 31.52; Carb: 8.4; Protein: 57.1

Pork and Apple Traybake

Prep Time: 15 Minutes   Cook Time: 40 Minutes   Serves: 4

Ingredients:

- 500g pork loin chops
- Salt and pepper to taste
- 2 tablespoons olive oil
- 2 apples, cored and sliced
- 2 red onions, cut into wedges
- 2 tablespoons wholegrain mustard
- 2 tablespoons honey
- Fresh thyme sprigs, for garnish

Directions:

1. Preheat one basket to Roast at 200°C for 5 minutes and choose the SYNC option.
2. Season the pork loin chops with salt and pepper.
3. Heat olive oil in the basket and sear the pork loin chops for 2-3 minutes on each side. Remove and set aside.
4. In the same basket, arrange sliced apples and onion wedges.
5. Nestle the seared pork loin chops among the apples and onions.
6. Drizzle wholegrain mustard and honey over the pork, apples, and onions.
7. Once the basket is preheated, roast for 30-35 minutes until the pork is cooked through and the apples are tender.
8. While the traybake is cooking, preheat the second basket to Air Fry at 180°C for 5 minutes.
9. Air fry some fresh thyme sprigs for 3-4 minutes until crispy.
10. Once the traybake is done, remove from the first basket and let rest for a

few minutes.

11. Serve the pork and apple traybake hot, garnished with crispy thyme sprigs.

Nutritional Value (Amount per Serving):

Calories: 434; Fat: 21.11; Carb: 28.48; Protein: 33.54

Pork and Leek Stuffed Bell Peppers

Prep Time: 20 Minutes   Cook Time: 30 Minutes   Serves: 4

Ingredients:

- 4 bell peppers, halved and deseeded
- 500g pork mince
- 2 leeks, finely chopped
- 2 cloves garlic, minced
- 100g cooked rice
- 1 teaspoon dried thyme
- Salt and pepper to taste
- 200ml passata
- 50g grated Cheddar cheese
- Fresh parsley, chopped, for garnish

Directions:

1. Preheat one basket to Bake at 180°C for 5 minutes and choose the SYNC option.
2. Place bell pepper halves in the basket in a single layer.
3. In a bowl, mix together pork mince, chopped leeks, minced garlic, cooked rice, dried thyme, salt, and pepper until well combined.
4. Stuff each bell pepper half with the pork and leek mixture.
5. Pour passata over the stuffed bell peppers.
6. Once the basket is preheated, bake for 25-30 minutes until the peppers are tender and the pork is cooked through.
7. While the stuffed bell peppers are baking, preheat the second basket to Air Fry at 180°C for 5 minutes.
8. Once the stuffed bell peppers are done, remove from the first basket and sprinkle grated Cheddar cheese over the top.
9. Air fry for 3-4 minutes in the second basket until the cheese is melted and bubbly.
10. Serve the pork and leek stuffed bell peppers hot, garnished with chopped fresh parsley.

Nutritional Value (Amount per Serving):

Calories: 425; Fat: 23.84; Carb: 16.74; Protein: 35.43

Beef Wellington

Prep Time: 30 Minutes   Cook Time: 45 Minutes   Serves: 4

Ingredients:

- 500g beef fillet
- Salt and pepper to taste
- 2 tablespoons olive oil
- 200g mushrooms, finely chopped
- 2 cloves garlic, minced
- 1 tablespoon fresh thyme leaves
- 320g puff pastry
- 2 tablespoons Dijon mustard
- 4 slices Parma ham
- 1 egg, beaten (for egg wash)

Directions:

1. Preheat the air fryer to Bake at 200°C for 5 minutes and choose the MATCH option.
2. Season the beef fillet with salt and pepper.
3. Heat olive oil in a skillet and sear the beef fillet on all sides until browned. Set aside to cool.
4. In the same baskets, bake mushrooms, garlic, and thyme until mushrooms release their moisture and become golden brown. Set aside to cool.
5. Roll out the puff pastry and spread Dijon mustard over the center.
6. Layer Parma ham slices on top of the mustard.
7. Spread the cooled mushroom mixture evenly over the Parma ham.
8. Place the seared beef fillet in the center of the pastry and fold the pastry over, sealing the edges.
9. Once the baskets are preheated, place the Beef Wellington seam side down.
10. Bake for 35-40 minutes until the pastry is golden brown and the beef is cooked to your desired doneness.
11. Once done, remove from the baskets and let rest for a few minutes before slicing.
12. Serve hot, accompanied by roasted vegetables and a red wine reduction sauce.

Nutritional Value (Amount per Serving):

Calories: 883; Fat: 48.35; Carb: 76.4; Protein: 43.05

Pork and Apple Burgers

Prep Time: 20 Minutes   Cook Time: 15 Minutes   Serves: 4

Ingredients:

- 500g pork mince
- 1 apple, grated
- 1 onion, grated
- 2 tablespoons breadcrumbs
- 1 teaspoon dried sage
- Salt and pepper to taste
- 4 burger buns

- Lettuce leaves, tomato slices, and sliced red onion for serving
- BBQ sauce or mayonnaise for topping

Directions:

1. Preheat one basket to roast at 200°C for 5 minutes and choose the SYNC option.
2. In a bowl, mix together pork mince, grated apple, grated onion, breadcrumbs, dried sage, salt, and pepper until well combined.
3. Divide the mixture into 4 equal portions and shape into burger patties.
4. Once the basket is preheated, place the burger patties in the basket.
5. Roast for 6-7 minutes on each side until cooked through and browned.
6. While the burgers are cooking, preheat the second basket to Air Fry at 180°C for 5 minutes.
7. Air fry the burger buns in the second basket for 2-3 minutes until lightly golden.
8. Once the burgers are done, remove from the first basket and let rest for a few minutes.
9. Serve the pork and apple burgers hot on toasted buns, topped with lettuce, tomato, sliced red onion, and your choice of BBQ sauce or mayonnaise.

Nutritional Value (Amount per Serving):

Calories: 639; Fat: 31.52; Carb: 42.05; Protein: 45.29

Lamb and Vegetable Skewers

Prep Time: 30 Minutes   Cook Time: 15 Minutes   Serves: 4

Ingredients:

- 500g lamb leg meat, cubed
- Salt and pepper to taste
- 2 tablespoons olive oil
- 2 cloves garlic, minced
- 1 tablespoon fresh rosemary, chopped
- 1 tablespoon fresh thyme leaves
- 2 zucchinis, sliced
- 1 red bell pepper, diced
- 1 yellow bell pepper, diced
- 1 red onion, diced
- Wooden skewers, soaked in water for 30 minutes

Directions:

1. Preheat the air fryer to roast at 200°C for 5 minutes and choose the MATCH option.
2. Season the lamb cubed with salt, pepper, minced garlic, chopped rosemary,

and thyme leaves. Let marinate for at least 30 minutes.
3. Thread marinated lamb cubes onto skewers, alternating with slices of zucchini, diced bell peppers, and red onion.
4. Once the baskets are preheated, place the skewers on the grill in a single layer.
5. Roast for 12-15 minutes, turning occasionally, until the lamb is cooked to your desired doneness and the vegetables are tender.
6. Once the skewers are done, remove from the baskets and let rest for a few minutes.
7. Serve the lamb and vegetable skewers hot, accompanied by couscous or a fresh salad.

Nutritional Value (Amount per Serving):

Calories: 241; Fat: 17.63; Carb: 6.66; Protein: 14.27

Pork and Apple Sausage Rolls

Prep Time: 20 Minutes   Cook Time: 25 Minutes   Serves: 4

Ingredients:

- 500g pork sausage meat
- 1 apple, grated
- 1 onion, finely chopped
- 2 tablespoons breadcrumbs
- 1 teaspoon dried sage
- Salt and pepper to taste
- 320g puff pastry
- 1 egg, beaten (for egg wash)
- Sesame seeds for topping (optional)

Directions:

1. Preheat the air fryer to Bake at 200°C for 5 minutes and choose the MATCH option.
2. In a bowl, mix together pork sausage meat, grated apple, chopped onion, breadcrumbs, dried sage, salt, and pepper until well combined.
3. Roll out the puff pastry and cut into rectangles.
4. Divide the sausage mixture into 4 portions and shape each portion into a long sausage shape.
5. Place each sausage shape onto a puff pastry rectangle and roll up, sealing the edges.
6. Once the baskets are preheated, place the sausage rolls seam side down.
7. Brush the tops of the sausage rolls with beaten egg and sprinkle with sesame seeds, if using.

8. Bake for 20-25 minutes until the pastry is golden brown and cooked through.
9. Once done, remove from the baskets and let cool slightly before serving.
10. Serve the pork and apple sausage rolls hot, accompanied by your favorite dipping sauce.

Nutritional Value (Amount per Serving):

Calories: 964; Fat: 71.45; Carb: 48.96; Protein: 33.36

Lamb and Mint Meatballs with Tomato Sauce

Prep Time: 30 Minutes   Cook Time: 25 Minutes   Serves: 4

Ingredients:

- 500g lamb mince
- 1 onion, grated
- 2 cloves garlic, minced
- 2 tablespoons fresh mint, chopped
- 2 tablespoons breadcrumbs
- 1 tablespoon olive oil
- 1 onion, chopped
- 2 cloves garlic, minced
- 400g canned chopped tomatoes
- 1 teaspoon dried oregano
- Salt and pepper to taste
- Fresh parsley, chopped, for garnish

Directions:

1. Preheat the baskets to Bake at 180°C for 5 minutes and choose the MATCH option.
2. In a bowl, mix together lamb mince, grated onion, minced garlic, chopped mint, breadcrumbs, salt, and pepper until well combined.
3. Roll the mixture into meatballs and place on a baking tray.
4. Once the baskets are preheated, place the meatballs in a single layer.
5. Bake for 20-25 minutes until cooked through and browned.
6. While the meatballs are baking, preheat the second basket to roast at 180°C for 5 minutes.
7. In a skillet, heat olive oil and roast chopped onion and minced garlic until softened.
8. Stir in canned chopped tomatoes, dried oregano, salt, and pepper. Roast for 10-15 minutes until the sauce thickens.
9. Once the meatballs are done, remove from the first basket and transfer to the tomato sauce.

10. Serve the lamb and mint meatballs hot, garnished with chopped fresh parsley, alongside pasta or crusty bread.

Nutritional Value (Amount per Serving):

Calories: 567; Fat: 33.55; Carb: 11.78; Protein: 53.03

Succulent Garlic Rosemary Lamb Chops

Prep Time: 10 Minutes   Cook Time: 20 Minutes   Serves: 4

Ingredients:

- 8 lamb chops
- 4 cloves garlic, minced
- 2 tablespoons fresh rosemary, chopped
- 2 tablespoons olive oil
- Salt and pepper to taste
- 1 lemon, sliced
- Fresh rosemary sprigs, for garnish

Directions:

1. Preheat one basket to Max Crisp at 200°C for 5 minutes and choose the SYNC option.
2. In a small bowl, mix together the minced garlic, chopped rosemary, olive oil, salt, and pepper to create a marinade.
3. Rub the lamb chops with the marinade, ensuring they are evenly coated.
4. Once the basket is preheated, place the lamb chops in a single layer.
5. Max Crisp for 10-12 minutes, flipping halfway through, until the lamb chops are browned and cooked to your desired doneness.
6. While the lamb chops are cooking, preheat the second basket to Roast at 180°C for 5 minutes.
7. Place lemon slices in the second basket.
8. Roast the lemon slices for 5 minutes until they are slightly caramelized.
9. Once the lamb chops are done, transfer them to a serving plate and cover with foil to keep warm.
10. Serve the succulent garlic rosemary lamb chops hot, garnished with roasted lemon slices and fresh rosemary sprigs.

Nutritional Value (Amount per Serving):

Calories: 1138; Fat: 58.49; Carb: 3.15; Protein: 150.35

Spicy Beef Tacos with Avocado Salsa

Prep Time: 20 Minutes   Cook Time: 15 Minutes   Serves: 4

Ingredients:

- 500g beef mince
- 2 tablespoons olive oil
- 1 onion, diced
- 2 cloves garlic, minced
- 1 tablespoon chili powder
- 1 teaspoon ground cumin
- 1 teaspoon paprika
- Salt and pepper to taste
- 2 ripe avocados, diced
- 1 tomato, diced
- 1/4 red onion, finely chopped
- 1 jalapeño, seeded and diced
- Juice of 1 lime
- 8 small corn tortillas
- Fresh coriander leaves, for garnish
- Lime wedges, for serving

Directions:

1. Preheat one basket to Air Fry at 200°C for 5 minutes and choose the SYNC option.
2. In a pan over medium heat, heat olive oil and sauté the diced onion and minced garlic until softened.
3. Add the beef mince and cook until browned, breaking it up with a spoon.
4. Stir in the chili powder, ground cumin, paprika, salt, and pepper. Cook for another 2-3 minutes.
5. Once the basket is preheated, transfer the beef mixture into it.
6. Air fry for 10-12 minutes until the beef is crispy and cooked through.
7. While the beef is cooking, prepare the avocado salsa by mixing together the diced avocados, tomato, red onion, jalapeño, lime juice, salt, and pepper in a bowl.
8. Preheat the second basket to Max Crisp at 180°C for 5 minutes.
9. Max crisp the corn tortillas in the second basket for 3-4 minutes until heated through.
10. Serve the spicy beef tacos by filling each warm tortilla with the crispy beef mixture and topping with avocado salsa and fresh coriander leaves.
11. Serve with lime wedges on the side for squeezing.

Nutritional Value (Amount per Serving):

Calories: 534; Fat: 30.65; Carb: 39.7; Protein: 31.96

Chapter 4: Fish and Seafood

Garlic and Herb Baked Salmon

Prep Time: 10 Minutes　　Cook Time: 15 Minutes　　Serves: 4

Ingredients:

- 4 salmon fillets
- 4 cloves garlic, minced
- 2 tablespoons chopped fresh parsley
- 1 tablespoon chopped fresh dill
- 2 tablespoons olive oil
- Salt and pepper to taste
- Lemon wedges, for serving

Directions:

1. Preheat the air fryer to bake at 180°C for 5 minutes and choose the MATCH option.
2. In a small bowl, mix minced garlic, chopped parsley, chopped dill, olive oil, salt, and pepper.
3. Place salmon fillets on baking trays lined with parchment paper.
4. Spread the garlic-herb mixture evenly over the salmon fillets.
5. Bake for 12-15 minutes until salmon is cooked through and flakes easily with a fork.
6. Serve hot with lemon wedges.

Nutritional Value (Amount per Serving):

Calories: 424; Fat: 23.33; Carb: 3.91; Protein: 47.57

Lemon and Herb Crusted Sea Bass

Prep Time: 10 Minutes　　Cook Time: 15 Minutes　　Serves: 4

Ingredients:

- 4 sea bass fillets
- Zest of 1 lemon
- 2 tablespoons chopped fresh parsley
- 1 tablespoon chopped fresh thyme
- 2 tablespoons olive oil
- Salt and pepper to taste
- Lemon wedges, for serving

Directions:

1. Preheat the air fryer to bake at 200°C for 5 minutes and choose the MATCH option.
2. In a bowl, mix lemon zest, chopped parsley, chopped thyme, olive oil, salt, and pepper.
3. Pat sea bass fillets dry and rub the herb mixture evenly over them.
4. Place sea bass fillets in the preheated baskets.

5. Bake for 12-15 minutes until fish is cooked through and flakes easily with a fork.
6. Serve hot with lemon wedges.

Nutritional Value (Amount per Serving):

Calories: 196; Fat: 9.44; Carb: 2.99; Protein: 24.17

Dehydrated Teriyaki Salmon Jerky

Prep Time: 10 Minutes   Cook Time: 4 Hours   Serves: 4

Ingredients:

- 500g salmon fillets, thinly sliced
- 4 tablespoons teriyaki sauce
- 2 tablespoons honey
- 1 tablespoon sesame seeds
- Pinch of salt

Directions:

1. In a bowl, mix teriyaki sauce, honey, sesame seeds, and a pinch of salt.
2. Add salmon slices to the marinade, ensuring they are evenly coated.
3. Preheat the air fryer to dehydrate at 70°C for 5 minutes and choose the MATCH option.
4. Arrange the marinated salmon slices in a single layer in the preheated baskets.
5. Dehydrate for 4 hours until the salmon is dried and jerky-like.
6. Serve as a tasty and nutritious snack.

Nutritional Value (Amount per Serving):

Calories: 447; Fat: 34.98; Carb: 11.69; Protein: 22.13

Max Crisp Breaded Haddock Fillets

Prep Time: 15 Minutes   Cook Time: 12 Minutes   Serves: 4

Ingredients:

- 4 haddock fillets
- 1 cup breadcrumbs
- 2 tablespoons grated Parmesan cheese
- 1 teaspoon dried parsley
- 1 teaspoon garlic powder
- Salt and pepper to taste
- Cooking spray

Directions:

1. Preheat the air fryer to max crisp at 200°C for 5 minutes and choose the

MATCH option.
2. In a shallow dish, mix breadcrumbs, Parmesan cheese, dried parsley, garlic powder, salt, and pepper.
3. Pat haddock fillets dry and coat them with the breadcrumb mixture.
4. Lightly spray both sides of the breaded fillets with cooking spray.
5. Place haddock fillets in the preheated baskets.
6. Max crisp for 10-12 minutes until the fillets are golden and crispy.
7. Serve hot with your favorite dipping sauce.

Nutritional Value (Amount per Serving):

Calories: 168; Fat: 1.64; Carb: 3.41; Protein: 32.85

Baked Garlic Butter Lobster Tails

Prep Time: 10 Minutes   Cook Time: 12 Minutes   Serves: 4

Ingredients:

- 4 lobster tails, thawed if frozen
- 4 tablespoons unsalted butter, melted
- 4 cloves garlic, minced
- 1 tablespoon chopped fresh parsley
- Salt and pepper to taste
- Lemon wedges, for serving

Directions:

1. Preheat the air fryer to bake at 200°C for 5 minutes and choose the MATCH option.
2. Using kitchen shears, carefully cut the top shell of each lobster tail lengthwise.
3. Gently lift the lobster meat and place it on top of the shell.
4. In a small bowl, mix melted butter, minced garlic, chopped parsley, salt, and pepper.
5. Brush the garlic butter mixture over the exposed lobster meat.
6. Place lobster tails in the preheated baskets.
7. Bake for 10-12 minutes until lobster meat is opaque and cooked through.
8. Serve hot with lemon wedges.

Nutritional Value (Amount per Serving):

Calories: 226; Fat: 11.87; Carb: 27.44; Protein: 4.35

Air Fryer Cajun Shrimp Skewers

Prep Time: 10 Minutes   Cook Time: 8 Minutes   Serves: 4

Ingredients:

- 500g large shrimp, peeled and deveined

- 2 tablespoons olive oil
- 1 tablespoon Cajun seasoning
- 1 teaspoon smoked paprika
- 1/2 teaspoon garlic powder
- 1/2 teaspoon onion powder
- Lemon wedges, for serving

Directions:

1. Preheat the air fryer to air fry at 200°C for 5 minutes and choose the MATCH option.
2. In a bowl, toss shrimp with olive oil, Cajun seasoning, smoked paprika, garlic powder, and onion powder until evenly coated.
3. Thread seasoned shrimp onto skewers.
4. Place shrimp skewers in the preheated baskets.
5. Air fry for 6-8 minutes until shrimp are pink and cooked through.
6. Serve hot with lemon wedges.

Nutritional Value (Amount per Serving):

Calories: 88; Fat: 7.06; Carb: 5.61; Protein: 1.05

Dehydrated Smoked Salmon

Prep Time: 10 Minutes   Cook Time: 4 Hours   Serves: 4

Ingredients:

- 500g smoked salmon slices
- 2 tablespoons maple syrup
- 1 tablespoon soy sauce
- 1 teaspoon liquid smoke (optional)

Directions:

1. In a bowl, mix maple syrup, soy sauce, and liquid smoke (if using).
2. Brush both sides of the smoked salmon slices with the maple syrup mixture.
3. Preheat the air fryer to dehydrate at 70°C for 5 minutes and choose the MATCH option.
4. Arrange the coated salmon slices in a single layer in the preheated baskets.
5. Dehydrate for 4 hours until the salmon is dried and slightly chewy.
6. Serve as a tasty snack or appetizer.

Nutritional Value (Amount per Serving):

Calories: 251; Fat: 11.69; Carb: 7.76; Protein: 26.93

Max Crisp Coconut Shrimp

Prep Time: 15 Minutes   Cook Time: 10 Minutes   Serves: 4

Ingredients:

- 500g large shrimp, peeled and deveined

- 1 cup shredded coconut
- 1 cup breadcrumbs
- 2 eggs, beaten
- Salt and pepper to taste
- Sweet chili sauce, for serving

Directions:

1. Preheat the air fryer to max crisp at 200°C for 5 minutes and choose the MATCH option.
2. In separate bowls, place shredded coconut, breadcrumbs, and beaten eggs.
3. Season shrimp with salt and pepper.
4. Dip each shrimp into the beaten eggs, then coat with shredded coconut and breadcrumbs mixture.
5. Place coated shrimp in the preheated baskets.
6. Max crisp for 8-10 minutes until shrimp are golden and crispy.
7. Serve hot with sweet chili sauce for dipping.

Nutritional Value (Amount per Serving):

Calories: 103; Fat: 5.18; Carb: 7.9; Protein: 6.06

Baked Lemon and Herb Stuffed Sole

Prep Time: 20 Minutes   Cook Time: 20 Minutes   Serves: 4

Ingredients:

- 4 sole fillets
- 1 cup breadcrumbs
- Zest of 1 lemon
- 2 tablespoons chopped fresh parsley
- 1 tablespoon chopped fresh dill
- 2 tablespoons unsalted butter, melted
- Salt and pepper to taste
- Lemon wedges, for serving

Directions:

1. Preheat the air fryer to bake at 180°C for 5 minutes and choose the MATCH option.
2. In a bowl, mix breadcrumbs, lemon zest, chopped parsley, chopped dill, melted butter, salt, and pepper.
3. Place a portion of the breadcrumb mixture onto each sole fillet and roll up.
4. Secure the rolled fillets with toothpicks if necessary.
5. Place stuffed sole fillets in the preheated baskets.
6. Bake for 18-20 minutes until fish is cooked through and breadcrumbs are golden.

7. Serve hot with lemon wedges.

Nutritional Value (Amount per Serving):

Calories: 165; Fat: 7.34; Carb: 3.75; Protein: 21.09

Air Fryer Coconut-Crusted Prawns

Prep Time: 15 Minutes   Cook Time: 10 Minutes   Serves: 4

Ingredients:

- 500g large prawns, peeled and deveined
- 1 cup shredded coconut
- 1 cup breadcrumbs
- 2 eggs, beaten
- Salt and pepper to taste
- Sweet chili sauce, for dipping

Directions:

1. Preheat the air fryer to air fry at 200°C for 5 minutes and choose the MATCH option.
2. In separate bowls, place shredded coconut and breadcrumbs.
3. Season prawns with salt and pepper.
4. Dip each prawn into the beaten eggs, then coat with the mixture of shredded coconut and breadcrumbs.
5. Place coated prawns in the preheated baskets.
6. Air fry for 8-10 minutes until prawns are golden and crispy.
7. Serve hot with sweet chili sauce for dipping.

Nutritional Value (Amount per Serving):

Calories: 103; Fat: 5.18; Carb: 7.9; Protein: 6.06

Baked Lemon Garlic Butter Scallops

Prep Time: 10 Minutes   Cook Time: 12 Minutes   Serves: 4

Ingredients:

- 500g scallops, cleaned and patted dry
- 4 tablespoons unsalted butter, melted
- 4 cloves garlic, minced
- Zest of 1 lemon
- 2 tablespoons chopped fresh parsley
- Salt and pepper to taste

Directions:

1. Preheat the air fryer to bake at 200°C for 5 minutes and choose the MATCH option.

2. In a bowl, mix melted butter, minced garlic, lemon zest, chopped parsley, salt, and pepper.
3. Arrange scallops in a single layer on baking trays lined with parchment paper.
4. Pour the garlic butter mixture over the scallops.
5. Place the baking trays in the preheated baskets.
6. Bake for 10-12 minutes until scallops are cooked through and lightly browned.
7. Serve hot, garnished with extra chopped parsley if desired.

Nutritional Value (Amount per Serving):

Calories: 168; Fat: 8.41; Carb: 6.98; Protein: 16.05

Dehydrated Teriyaki Tuna Jerky

Prep Time: 15 Minutes   Cook Time: 4 Hours   Serves: 4

Ingredients:

- 500g tuna steaks, thinly sliced
- 4 tablespoons teriyaki sauce
- 2 tablespoons honey
- 1 tablespoon sesame seeds
- Pinch of salt

Directions:

1. In a bowl, mix teriyaki sauce, honey, sesame seeds, and a pinch of salt.
2. Brush both sides of the tuna slices with the teriyaki mixture.
3. Preheat the air fryer to dehydrate at 70°C for 5 minutes and choose the MATCH option.
4. Arrange the coated tuna slices in a single layer in the preheated baskets.
5. Dehydrate for 4 hours until the tuna is dried and slightly chewy.
6. Serve as a delicious and nutritious snack.

Nutritional Value (Amount per Serving):

Calories: 447; Fat: 34.98; Carb: 11.69; Protein: 22.13

Max Crisp Breaded Mackerel Fillets

Prep Time: 15 Minutes   Cook Time: 12 Minutes   Serves: 4

Ingredients:

- 4 mackerel fillets
- 1 cup breadcrumbs
- 2 tablespoons grated Parmesan cheese
- 1 teaspoon dried oregano
- 1 teaspoon smoked paprika
- Salt and pepper to taste
- Cooking spray

Directions:

1. Preheat the air fryer to max crisp at 200°C for 5 minutes and choose the MATCH option.
2. In a shallow dish, mix breadcrumbs, Parmesan cheese, oregano, smoked paprika, salt, and pepper.
3. Pat mackerel fillets dry and coat them with the breadcrumb mixture.
4. Lightly spray both sides of the breaded fillets with cooking spray.
5. Place mackerel fillets in the preheated baskets.
6. Max crisp for 10-12 minutes until fillets are golden and crispy.
7. Serve hot with your favorite sauce or side dish.

Nutritional Value (Amount per Serving):

Calories: 440; Fat: 8.77; Carb: 3.3; Protein: 81.62

Air Fryer Garlic Herb Salmon

Prep Time: 10 Minutes   Cook Time: 10 Minutes   Serves: 4

Ingredients:

- 4 salmon fillets
- 2 tablespoons olive oil
- 4 cloves garlic, minced
- 2 tablespoons chopped fresh parsley
- 1 tablespoon chopped fresh dill
- Salt and pepper to taste
- Lemon wedges, for serving

Directions:

1. Preheat the air fryer to air fry at 200°C for 5 minutes and choose the MATCH option.
2. In a small bowl, mix olive oil, minced garlic, chopped parsley, chopped dill, salt, and pepper.
3. Rub the garlic herb mixture over each salmon fillet.
4. Place the salmon fillets in the preheated baskets.
5. Air fry for 8-10 minutes until the salmon is cooked through and flakes easily with a fork.
6. Serve hot with lemon wedges.

Nutritional Value (Amount per Serving):

Calories: 424; Fat: 23.33; Carb: 3.91; Protein: 47.57

Baked Lemon Butter Haddock

Prep Time: 10 Minutes   Cook Time: 15 Minutes   Serves: 4

Ingredients:

- 4 haddock fillets
- 4 tablespoons unsalted butter, melted
- Zest of 1 lemon
- Juice of 1 lemon
- 2 cloves garlic, minced
- Salt and pepper to taste
- Fresh parsley, chopped, for garnish

Directions:

1. Preheat the air fryer to bake at 180°C for 5 minutes and choose the MATCH option.
2. In a small bowl, mix melted butter, lemon zest, lemon juice, minced garlic, salt, and pepper.
3. Place haddock fillets on baking trays lined with parchment paper.
4. Pour the lemon butter mixture over the haddock fillets.
5. Place the baking trays in the preheated baskets.
6. Bake for 12-15 minutes until the haddock is cooked through and flakes easily with a fork.
7. Garnish with chopped parsley before serving.

Nutritional Value (Amount per Serving):

Calories: 230; Fat: 8.79; Carb: 4.17; Protein: 32.81

Max Crisp Lemon Pepper Cod

Prep Time: 10 Minutes   Cook Time: 12 Minutes   Serves: 4

Ingredients:

- 4 cod fillets
- 2 tablespoons olive oil
- Zest of 1 lemon
- 1 teaspoon cracked black pepper
- Salt to taste
- Lemon wedges, for serving

Directions:

1. Preheat the air fryer to max crisp at 200°C for 5 minutes and choose the MATCH option.
2. In a small bowl, mix olive oil, lemon zest, cracked black pepper, and salt.
3. Rub the lemon pepper mixture over each cod fillet.
4. Place the cod fillets in the preheated baskets.
5. Max crisp for 10-12 minutes until the cod is cooked through and flakes easily with a fork.
6. Serve hot with lemon wedges. Enjoy your flavorful lemon pepper cod!

Nutritional Value (Amount per Serving):

Calories: 147; Fat: 7.31; Carb: 2.12; Protein: 17.87

Baked Garlic and Herb Butter Prawns

Prep Time: 15 Minutes   Cook Time: 10 Minutes   Serves: 4

Ingredients:

- 500g large prawns, peeled and deveined
- 4 tablespoons unsalted butter, melted
- 4 cloves garlic, minced
- 2 tablespoons chopped fresh parsley
- 1 tablespoon chopped fresh thyme
- Salt and pepper to taste
- Lemon wedges, for serving

Directions:

1. Preheat the air fryer to bake at 200°C for 5 minutes and choose the MATCH option.
2. In a small bowl, mix melted butter, minced garlic, chopped parsley, chopped thyme, salt, and pepper.
3. Place the prawns in baking dishes or on baking trays.
4. Pour the garlic herb butter mixture over the prawns, ensuring they are evenly coated.
5. Place the baking dishes or trays in the preheated baskets.
6. Bake for 8-10 minutes until the prawns are pink and cooked through.
7. Serve hot with lemon wedges.

Nutritional Value (Amount per Serving):

Calories: 98; Fat: 8.01; Carb: 5.85; Protein: 1.75

Max Crisp Lemon and Herb Seabass

Prep Time: 10 Minutes   Cook Time: 12 Minutes   Serves: 4

Ingredients:

- 4 seabass fillets
- 2 tablespoons olive oil
- Zest of 1 lemon
- 2 tablespoons chopped fresh parsley
- 1 tablespoon chopped fresh thyme
- Salt and pepper to taste
- Lemon wedges, for serving

Directions:

1. Preheat the air fryer to max crisp at 200°C for 5 minutes and choose the MATCH option.
2. In a small bowl, mix olive oil, lemon zest, chopped parsley, chopped thyme, salt, and pepper.
3. Pat the seabass fillets dry with paper towels.

4. Rub the lemon herb mixture over each seabass fillet, ensuring they are evenly coated.
5. Place the seabass fillets in the preheated baskets.
6. Max crisp for 10-12 minutes until the fillets are cooked through and crispy on the outside.
7. Serve hot with lemon wedges. Enjoy the flavorful and crispy lemon herb seabass!

Nutritional Value (Amount per Serving):

Calories: 317; Fat: 22.16; Carb: 10.64; Protein: 19.95

Fish and Chips

Prep Time: 15 Minutes   Cook Time: 20 Minutes   Serves: 4

Ingredients:

- 4 fillets of white fish (such as cod or haddock), skin removed
- 2 large potatoes, peeled and cut into thick chips
- 2 tablespoons olive oil
- 1 teaspoon garlic powder
- 1 teaspoon paprika
- Salt and pepper to taste
- Lemon wedges, for serving
- Tartar sauce, for serving

Directions:

1. Preheat one basket to roast at 200°C for 5 minutes and choose the SYNC option.
2. In a bowl, toss the potato chips with olive oil, garlic powder, paprika, salt, and pepper until evenly coated.
3. Spread the potato chips evenly in the preheated basket.
4. Roast for 15-20 minutes, shaking the basket halfway through, until the chips are golden and crispy.
5. At the same time, preheat the second basket to air fry at 200°C for 5 minutes.
6. Season the fish fillets with salt and pepper.
7. Place the fish fillets in the preheated second basket.
8. Air fry the fish for 8-10 minutes, depending on the thickness of the fillets, until they are golden and cooked through.
9. Once the chips are done, remove them from the first basket and set aside.
10. Serve the fish and chips hot, with lemon wedges and tartar sauce on the side.

Nutritional Value (Amount per Serving):

Calories: 283; Fat: 7.21; Carb: 53.4; Protein: 4.99

Chapter 5: Vegetables and Sides

Balsamic Glazed Roasted Vegetables

Prep Time: 15 Minutes   Cook Time: 25 Minutes   Serves: 4

Ingredients:

- 2 carrots, peeled and cut into sticks
- 2 parsnips, peeled and cut into sticks
- 1 red onion, cut into wedges
- 1 tablespoon olive oil
- 2 tablespoons balsamic vinegar
- 1 tablespoon honey
- 1 teaspoon dried rosemary
- Salt and pepper to taste
- 50g walnuts, chopped
- Fresh parsley, for garnish

Directions:

1. Preheat the air fryer to roast at 200°C for 5 minutes and choose the MATCH option.
2. In a large mixing bowl, toss together the carrots, parsnips, red onion, olive oil, balsamic vinegar, honey, dried rosemary, salt, and pepper until well coated.
3. Once the baskets are preheated, spread the vegetable mixture evenly in the baskets.
4. Roast for 20-25 minutes, stirring halfway through, until the vegetables are tender and caramelized.
5. Once the vegetables are done, remove them from the baskets.
6. Transfer the roasted vegetables to serving dishes and sprinkle chopped walnuts over the top.
7. Garnish with fresh parsley and serve hot as a delightful side dish.

Nutritional Value (Amount per Serving):

Calories: 197; Fat: 11.84; Carb: 22.09; Protein: 3.5

Garlic Herb Hasselback Potatoes

Prep Time: 15 Minutes   Cook Time: 40 Minutes   Serves: 4

Ingredients:

- 4 large potatoes, scrubbed
- 3 tablespoons melted butter
- 3 cloves garlic, minced
- 2 tablespoons chopped fresh herbs (such as rosemary, thyme, or parsley)

- Salt and pepper to taste
- Grated Parmesan cheese for topping

Directions:

1. Preheat the air fryer to bake at 200°C for 5 minutes and choose the MATCH option.
2. Place a potato on a cutting board, flat side down. Make thin slices across the potato, being careful not to cut all the way through, leaving about 1/8 inch intact.
3. In a small bowl, mix together the melted butter, minced garlic, chopped fresh herbs, salt, and pepper.
4. Once the basket is preheated, place the potatoes in the baskets.
5. Brush the garlic herb butter mixture over the potatoes, making sure to get it in between the slices.
6. Bake for 35-40 minutes until the potatoes are tender and golden brown, brushing with more butter halfway through.
7. Once the potatoes are done, remove them from the baskets.
8. Sprinkle grated Parmesan cheese over the potatoes and serve hot as a flavorful side dish.

Nutritional Value (Amount per Serving):

Calories: 398; Fat: 9.37; Carb: 69.97; Protein: 10.79

Stuffed Bell Peppers

Prep Time: 20 Minutes   Cook Time: 25 Minutes   Serves: 4

Ingredients:

- 4 large bell peppers, any color
- 200g cooked quinoa
- 200g canned black beans, drained and rinsed
- 1 cup corn kernels
- 1 red onion, diced
- 2 cloves garlic, minced
- 1 teaspoon ground cumin
- 1 teaspoon chili powder
- Salt and pepper to taste
- 100g grated cheddar cheese
- Fresh coriander, for garnish

Directions:

1. Preheat one basket to roast at 200°C for 5 minutes and choose the SYNC option.
2. Cut the tops off the bell peppers and remove the seeds and membranes.

3. In a large mixing bowl, combine the cooked quinoa, black beans, corn kernels, diced red onion, minced garlic, ground cumin, chili powder, salt, and pepper.
4. Once the basket is preheated, stuff the bell peppers with the quinoa mixture and place them in the basket.
5. Roast for 20-25 minutes until the peppers are tender and slightly charred.
6. While the peppers are roasting, preheat the second basket to air fry at 180°C for 5 minutes.
7. Once the peppers are done, remove them from the first basket.
8. Sprinkle grated cheddar cheese over the stuffed peppers and air fry for 5 minutes on the second basket until the cheese is melted and bubbly.
9. Garnish with fresh coriander and serve hot as a satisfying vegetarian main or side dish.

Nutritional Value (Amount per Serving):

Calories: 240; Fat: 4.41; Carb: 40.57; Protein: 12.79

Butternut Squash Risotto

Prep Time: 15 Minutes   Cook Time: 25 Minutes   Serves: 4

Ingredients:

- 500g butternut squash, peeled, seeded, and diced
- 2 tablespoons olive oil
- Salt and pepper to taste
- 1 onion, finely chopped
- 2 cloves garlic, minced
- 300g Arborio rice
- 120ml dry white wine
- 1 litre vegetable broth, heated
- 50g grated Parmesan cheese
- 2 tablespoons chopped fresh sage leaves

Directions:

1. Preheat the air fryer to roast at 200°C for 5 minutes and choose the MATCH option.
2. In a large mixing bowl, toss together the diced butternut squash, olive oil, salt, and pepper until well coated.
3. Once the basket is preheated, spread the butternut squash evenly in the baskets.
4. Roast for 20-25 minutes, stirring halfway through, until the squash is tender and caramelized.
5. In a separate saucepan, heat some olive oil over medium heat. Add the

chopped onion and minced garlic and cook until softened.

6. Stir in the Arborio rice and cook for 2 minutes until translucent.
7. Pour in the white wine and cook until absorbed, stirring constantly.
8. Gradually add the hot vegetable broth, a ladleful at a time, stirring constantly until the liquid is absorbed before adding more.
9. Once the rice is creamy and cooked through, stir in the roasted butternut squash, grated Parmesan cheese, and chopped fresh sage leaves.
10. Serve with extra Parmesan cheese and sage leaves, if desired.

Nutritional Value (Amount per Serving):

Calories: 2472; Fat: 268.17; Carb: 28.54; Protein: 12.69

Roasted Garlic Cauliflower Mash

Prep Time: 10 Minutes   Cook Time: 25 Minutes   Serves: 4

Ingredients:

- 1 large head of cauliflower, cut into florets
- 4 cloves garlic, peeled
- 2 tablespoons olive oil
- Salt and pepper to taste
- 2 tablespoons butter
- 50ml milk or vegetable broth
- Chopped chives for garnish

Directions:

1. Preheat the air fryer to roast at 200°C for 5 minutes and choose the MATCH option.
2. In a large mixing bowl, toss together the cauliflower florets, whole garlic cloves, olive oil, salt, and pepper until well coated.
3. Once the baskets are preheated, spread the cauliflower and garlic evenly in the baskets.
4. Roast for 20-25 minutes, shaking the basket halfway through, until the cauliflower is tender and golden brown.
5. Once the cauliflower is done, remove it from the baskets.
6. Transfer the roasted cauliflower and garlic to a food processor or blender.
7. Add the butter and milk or vegetable broth, then blend until smooth and creamy.
8. Serve the roasted garlic cauliflower mash hot, garnished with chopped chives.

Nutritional Value (Amount per Serving):

Calories: 137; Fat: 12.73; Carb: 5.55; Protein: 1.76

Lemon Garlic Green Beans

Prep Time: 10 Minutes   Cook Time: 15 Minutes   Serves: 4

Ingredients:

- 400g green beans, trimmed
- 2 tablespoons olive oil
- 2 cloves garlic, minced
- Zest and juice of 1 lemon
- Salt and pepper to taste
- Sliced almonds for garnish

Directions:

1. Preheat the air fryer to roast at 200°C for 5 minutes and choose the MATCH option.
2. In a large mixing bowl, toss together the green beans, olive oil, minced garlic, lemon zest, lemon juice, salt, and pepper until evenly coated.
3. Once the baskets are preheated, spread the green beans evenly in the baskets.
4. Roast for 12-15 minutes until the green beans are tender and slightly caramelized, shaking the baskets halfway through.
5. Once the green beans are done, remove them from the baskets.
6. Transfer the roasted green beans to a serving dish and sprinkle sliced almonds over the top.
7. Serve the lemon garlic green beans hot as a vibrant and flavorful side dish.

Nutritional Value (Amount per Serving):

Calories: 93; Fat: 7.42; Carb: 6.77; Protein: 1.55

Sweet Potato Fries

Prep Time: 10 Minutes   Cook Time: 20 Minutes   Serves: 4

Ingredients:

- 2 large sweet potatoes, peeled and cut into fries
- 2 tablespoons cornflour
- 2 tablespoons olive oil
- 1 teaspoon smoked paprika
- 1/2 teaspoon garlic powder
- Salt and pepper to taste

Directions:

1. Preheat the air fryer to air fry at 200°C for 5 minutes and choose the MATCH option.
2. In a large mixing bowl, toss together the sweet potato fries, cornflour, olive oil, smoked paprika, garlic powder, salt, and pepper until evenly coated.
3. Once the baskets are preheated, spread the sweet potato fries evenly in the

baskets.

4. Air fry for 15-20 minutes, shaking the basket halfway through, until the fries are crispy and golden brown.
5. Once the sweet potato fries are done, remove them from the baskets.
6. Transfer the crispy sweet potato fries to a serving dish and serve hot as a delicious side or snack.

Nutritional Value (Amount per Serving):

Calories: 148; Fat: 6.98; Carb: 20.3; Protein: 2.18

Garlic Herb Roasted Asparagus

Prep Time: 10 Minutes   Cook Time: 15 Minutes   Serves: 4

Ingredients:

- 500g asparagus spears, trimmed
- 2 tablespoons olive oil
- 2 cloves garlic, minced
- 1 tablespoon chopped fresh parsley
- 1 tablespoon chopped fresh thyme
- Salt and pepper to taste
- Lemon wedges for serving

Directions:

1. Preheat the air fryer to roast at 200°C for 5 minutes and choose the MATCH option.
2. In a large mixing bowl, toss together the asparagus spears, olive oil, minced garlic, chopped fresh parsley, chopped fresh thyme, salt, and pepper until evenly coated.
3. Once the baskets are preheated, spread the asparagus spears evenly in the baskets.
4. Roast for 12-15 minutes until the asparagus is tender and slightly charred, shaking the basket halfway through.
5. Once the asparagus is done, remove it from the baskets.
6. Transfer the roasted asparagus to a serving dish and serve hot with lemon wedges for squeezing over the top.

Nutritional Value (Amount per Serving):

Calories: 95; Fat: 6.98; Carb: 7.44; Protein: 3.17

Roasted Beetroot Salad

Prep Time: 15 Minutes   Cook Time: 45 Minutes   Serves: 4

Ingredients:

- 500g beetroot, peeled and cut into wedges

- 2 tablespoons olive oil
- 2 tablespoons balsamic vinegar
- 1 tablespoon honey
- 100g feta cheese, crumbled
- 50g walnuts, chopped
- Fresh rocket leaves for serving
- Salt and pepper to taste

Directions:

1. Preheat the air fryer to roast at 200°C for 5 minutes and choose the MATCH option.
2. In a large mixing bowl, toss together the beetroot wedges, olive oil, balsamic vinegar, honey, salt, and pepper until evenly coated.
3. Once the basket is preheated, spread the beetroot wedges evenly in the baskets.
4. Roast for 40-45 minutes until the beetroot is tender and caramelized, stirring occasionally.
5. Once the beetroot is done, remove it from the baskets.
6. Transfer the roasted beetroot to a serving platter and sprinkle crumbled feta cheese and chopped walnuts over the top.
7. Serve the roasted beetroot salad on a bed of fresh rocket leaves, drizzling any remaining juices from the pan over the top.

Nutritional Value (Amount per Serving):

Calories: 462; Fat: 34.04; Carb: 10.91; Protein: 30.44

Creamy Garlic Mushrooms

Prep Time: 10 Minutes   Cook Time: 15 Minutes   Serves: 4

Ingredients:

- 500g mushrooms, sliced
- 2 tablespoons butter
- 3 cloves garlic, minced
- 120ml double cream
- 2 tablespoons chopped fresh parsley
- Salt and pepper to taste
- Crusty bread for serving

Directions:

1. Preheat the air fryer to roast at 200°C for 5 minutes and choose the MATCH option.
2. In a large skillet, melt the butter over medium heat.
3. Add the sliced mushrooms and minced garlic, cooking until the mushrooms are tender and golden brown.
4. Once the baskets are preheated, transfer the cooked mushrooms to oven-safe dishes.

5. Pour the double cream over the mushrooms and stir to combine.
6. Sprinkle chopped fresh parsley over the top and season with salt and pepper to taste.
7. Roast for 10-12 minutes until the sauce is bubbling and slightly thickened.
8. Serve the creamy garlic mushrooms hot, with crusty bread for dipping.

Nutritional Value (Amount per Serving):

Calories: 504; Fat: 12.76; Carb: 100.69; Protein: 13.85

Crispy Brussels Sprouts with Balsamic Glaze

Prep Time: 10 Minutes   Cook Time: 20 Minutes   Serves: 4

Ingredients:

- 500g Brussels sprouts, trimmed and halved
- 2 tablespoons olive oil
- Salt and pepper to taste
- 2 tablespoons balsamic glaze

Directions:

1. Preheat the air fryer to Max Crisp at 200°C for 5 minutes and choose the MATCH option.
2. In a large mixing bowl, toss together the Brussels sprouts, olive oil, salt, and pepper until evenly coated.
3. Once the baskets are preheated, spread the Brussels sprouts evenly in the baskets.
4. Max crisp for 15-20 minutes until the Brussels sprouts are crispy and golden brown, shaking the baskets halfway through.
5. Once the Brussels sprouts are done, remove them from the baskets.
6. Drizzle the cooked Brussels sprouts with balsamic glaze before serving hot as a delicious side dish.

Nutritional Value (Amount per Serving):

Calories: 128; Fat: 7.25; Carb: 14.55; Protein: 5.07

Air Fried Butternut Squash Wedges

Prep Time: 15 Minutes   Cook Time: 25 Minutes   Serves: 4

Ingredients:

- 1 medium butternut squash, peeled, seeded, and cut into wedges
- 2 tablespoons olive oil
- 1 teaspoon smoked paprika
- 1/2 teaspoon garlic powder
- Salt and pepper to taste

Directions:

1. Preheat the air fryer to Air Fry at 200°C for 5 minutes and choose the MATCH option.
2. In a large mixing bowl, toss together the butternut squash wedges, olive oil, smoked paprika, garlic powder, salt, and pepper until evenly coated.
3. Once the baskets are preheated, spread the butternut squash wedges evenly in the baskets.
4. Air fry for 20-25 minutes until the squash is tender and caramelized, shaking the baskets halfway through.
5. Once the butternut squash is done, remove them from the baskets.
6. Serve the air-fried butternut squash wedges hot as a flavorful and healthy side dish.

Nutritional Value (Amount per Serving):

Calories: 292; Fat: 7.35; Carb: 60.12; Protein: 5.37

Baked Parmesan Zucchini Chips

Prep Time: 15 Minutes   Cook Time: 25 Minutes   Serves: 4

Ingredients:

- 2 large zucchinis, thinly sliced
- 1/2 cup grated Parmesan cheese
- 1/2 teaspoon garlic powder
- 1/2 teaspoon dried oregano
- Salt and pepper to taste
- Cooking spray

Directions:

1. Preheat the air fryer to Bake at 180°C for 5 minutes and choose the MATCH option.
2. In a shallow dish, combine the grated Parmesan cheese, garlic powder, dried oregano, salt, and pepper.
3. Dip each zucchini slice into the Parmesan mixture, coating both sides evenly.
4. Once the baskets are preheated, arrange the coated zucchini slices in a single layer in the baskets, ensuring they are not overlapping.
5. Lightly spray the zucchini slices with cooking spray.
6. Bake for 20-25 minutes until the zucchini slices are crispy and golden brown.
7. Once the zucchini chips are done, remove them from the baskets.
8. Serve the baked Parmesan zucchini chips hot as a crunchy and flavorful snack or side dish.

Nutritional Value (Amount per Serving):

Calories: 1117; Fat: 95.41; Carb: 4.59; Protein: 60.26

Rosemary Garlic Roasted Potatoes

Prep Time: 15 Minutes   Cook Time: 35 Minutes   Serves: 4

Ingredients:

- 800g baby potatoes, halved
- 3 tablespoons olive oil
- 3 cloves garlic, minced
- 1 tablespoon chopped fresh rosemary
- Salt and pepper to taste

Directions:

1. Preheat the air fryer to Max Crisp at 200°C for 5 minutes and choose the MATCH option.
2. In a large mixing bowl, toss together the halved baby potatoes, olive oil, minced garlic, chopped fresh rosemary, salt, and pepper until evenly coated.
3. Once the baskets are preheated, spread the potatoes evenly in the baskets.
4. Cook for 30-35 minutes until the potatoes are crispy and golden brown, shaking the baskets halfway through.
5. Once the potatoes are done, remove them from the baskets.
6. Serve the rosemary garlic roasted potatoes hot as a delicious and aromatic side dish.

Nutritional Value (Amount per Serving):

Calories: 252; Fat: 10.36; Carb: 36.84; Protein: 4.42

Baked Sweetcorn Fritters

Prep Time: 15 Minutes   Cook Time: 20 Minutes   Serves: 4

Ingredients:

- 300g sweetcorn kernels (fresh or frozen)
- 1 red pepper, finely chopped
- 2 spring onions, finely chopped
- 100g plain flour
- 2 eggs, beaten
- 1 teaspoon baking powder
- Salt and pepper to taste
- Cooking spray

Directions:

1. Preheat the air fryer to Bake at 180°C for 5 minutes and choose the MATCH option.

2. In a large mixing bowl, combine the sweetcorn kernels, chopped red pepper, chopped spring onions, plain flour, beaten eggs, baking powder, salt, and pepper until well combined.
3. Once the basket is preheated, lightly grease it with cooking spray.
4. Spoon the sweetcorn mixture onto the basket to form fritters, leaving some space between each.
5. Bake for 18-20 minutes until the fritters are golden and cooked through.
6. Once the fritters are done, remove them from the baskets.
7. Serve the baked sweetcorn fritters hot as a tasty and satisfying side dish.

Nutritional Value (Amount per Serving):

Calories: 274; Fat: 6.27; Carb: 43.59; Protein: 10.63

Dehydrated Apple Chips

Prep Time: 10 Minutes   Cook Time: 4-6 Hours   Serves: 4

Ingredients:

- 4 large apples, cored and thinly sliced
- 1 tablespoon lemon juice
- Cinnamon (optional)

Directions:

1. Preheat the air fryer to Dehydrate at 70°C for 5 minutes and choose the MATCH option.
2. In a large mixing bowl, toss the thinly sliced apples with lemon juice to prevent browning.
3. Once the baskets are preheated, arrange the apple slices in a single layer in the baskets.
4. Dehydrate for 4-6 hours until the apple slices are crisp, checking periodically for desired texture.
5. Once the apple chips are done, remove them from the baskets.
6. Sprinkle with cinnamon if desired and serve the dehydrated apple chips as a healthy and delicious snack or side.

Nutritional Value (Amount per Serving):

Calories: 155; Fat: 0.97; Carb: 40.34; Protein: 0.66

Stuffed Portobello Mushrooms

Prep Time: 15 Minutes   Cook Time: 20 Minutes   Serves: 4

Ingredients:

- 4 large Portobello mushrooms
- 200g spinach, chopped

- 1 red bell pepper, diced
- 2 cloves garlic, minced
- 100g feta cheese, crumbled
- 2 tablespoons olive oil
- Salt and pepper to taste
- Fresh parsley for garnish

Directions:

1. Preheat the air fryer to Bake at 180°C for 5 minutes and choose the MATCH option.
2. Remove the stems from the Portobello mushrooms and scoop out the gills to create a cavity.
3. In a skillet, heat olive oil over medium heat. Add minced garlic and diced red bell pepper, sautéing until softened.
4. Add chopped spinach to the skillet and cook until wilted. Season with salt and pepper to taste.
5. Once the baskets are preheated, arrange the Portobello mushrooms in the baskets.
6. Fill each mushroom cavity with the cooked spinach mixture and top with crumbled feta cheese.
7. Bake for 15-20 minutes until the mushrooms are tender and the cheese is melted.
8. Serve the stuffed Portobello mushrooms hot, garnished with fresh parsley.

Nutritional Value (Amount per Serving):

Calories: 184; Fat: 13.03; Carb: 10.95; Protein: 9.46

Chapter 6: Appetizers and Snacks

Crispy Scotch Eggs with Mustard Sauce

Prep Time: 20 Minutes   Cook Time: 15 Minutes   Serves: 4

Ingredients:

- 4 large eggs
- 400g sausage meat
- 100g breadcrumbs
- 1 teaspoon dried sage
- 1/2 teaspoon garlic powder
- Flour for coating

- 2 tablespoons vegetable oil
- 1/4 cup (60ml) mayonnaise
- 2 tablespoons Dijon mustard
- 1 tablespoon honey
- Salt and pepper to taste

Directions:

1. Preheat Air Fryer to Max Crisp at 180°C for 5 minutes and choose the MATCH option.
2. Boil eggs for 6 minutes, then transfer to cold water and peel.
3. In a bowl, mix sausage meat with dried sage, garlic powder, salt, and pepper.
4. Divide sausage meat into 4 portions and flatten each portion.
5. Place a peeled egg in the center of each portion and wrap the sausage meat around the egg, ensuring it's evenly covered.
6. Roll each sausage-coated egg in flour, then dip in beaten egg, and coat with breadcrumbs.
7. Lightly spray each scotch egg with cooking spray.
8. Max Crisp for 12-15 minutes until golden and crispy.
9. While the scotch eggs are cooking, mix mayonnaise, Dijon mustard, honey, salt, and pepper to make the mustard sauce.
10. Serve the crispy scotch eggs hot with mustard sauce on the side.

Nutritional Value (Amount per Serving):

Calories: 549; Fat: 34.83; Carb: 38.78; Protein: 25.66

Sticky BBQ Chicken Wings

Prep Time: 15 Minutes   Cook Time: 20 Minutes   Serves: 4

Ingredients:

- 12 chicken wings
- 1/2 cup (120ml) BBQ sauce
- 2 tablespoons soy sauce
- 2 tablespoons honey
- 1 tablespoon olive oil

- 1 teaspoon garlic powder
- Salt and pepper to taste
- Sesame seeds and chopped spring onions for garnish

Directions:

1. Preheat Air Fryer to Air Fry at 200°C for 5 minutes and choose the MATCH

option.

2. In a bowl, mix BBQ sauce, soy sauce, honey, olive oil, garlic powder, salt, and pepper.
3. Add chicken wings to the bowl and toss until evenly coated.
4. Arrange chicken wings in a single layer in the preheated baskets.
5. Air fry for 18-20 minutes, flipping halfway through, until cooked through and crispy.
6. Serve hot, garnished with sesame seeds and chopped spring onions.

Nutritional Value (Amount per Serving):

Calories: 256; Fat: 12.33; Carb: 15.28; Protein: 22.02

Crispy Halloumi Fries with Tzatziki Dip

Prep Time: 15 Minutes   Cook Time: 10 Minutes   Serves: 4

Ingredients:

- 250g halloumi cheese, cut into fries
- 1/2 cup (60g) flour
- 2 eggs, beaten
- 1 cup (120g) breadcrumbs
- 1 teaspoon dried oregano
- 1/2 teaspoon garlic powder
- Cooking spray
- 1/2 cucumber, grated and squeezed to remove excess moisture
- 1 cup (240ml) Greek yogurt
- 1 garlic clove, minced
- 1 tablespoon chopped fresh dill
- Salt and pepper to taste

Directions:

1. Preheat Air Fryer to Max Crisp at 200°C for 5 minutes and choose the MATCH option.
2. Set up three shallow dishes: one with flour, one with beaten eggs, and one with breadcrumbs mixed with dried oregano, garlic powder, salt, and pepper.
3. Dredge halloumi fries in flour, then dip in beaten eggs, and coat with breadcrumb mixture.
4. Arrange coated halloumi fries in a single layer in the preheated baskets.
5. Lightly spray the halloumi fries with cooking spray.
6. Max Crisp for 8-10 minutes until golden and crispy.
7. While the halloumi fries are cooking, prepare the tzatziki dip by mixing grated cucumber, Greek yogurt, minced garlic, chopped fresh dill, salt, and

pepper in a bowl.

8. Serve the crispy halloumi fries hot with tzatziki dip on the side.

Nutritional Value (Amount per Serving):

Calories: 359; Fat: 20.41; Carb: 19.83; Protein: 24.01

Savoury Cheese and Herb Scones

Prep Time: 15 Minutes   Cook Time: 12 Minutes   Serves: 4

Ingredients:

- 250g self-raising flour
- 1 teaspoon baking powder
- 50g unsalted butter, cold and cubed
- 100g mature cheddar cheese, grated
- 1 tablespoon chopped fresh chives
- 1 tablespoon chopped fresh parsley
- 150ml milk
- Salt and pepper to taste

Directions:

1. Preheat Air Fryer to Bake at 180°C for 5 minutes and choose the MATCH option.
2. In a large bowl, sift self-raising flour and baking powder together.
3. Rub in cold cubed butter until the mixture resembles breadcrumbs.
4. Stir in grated cheddar cheese, chopped fresh chives, chopped fresh parsley, salt, and pepper.
5. Gradually add milk and mix until a soft dough forms.
6. Turn the dough out onto a floured surface and pat into a 2cm thick round.
7. Use a floured cutter to cut out scones and place them on a baking tray.
8. Arrange scones in a single layer in the preheated baskets.
9. Bake for 10-12 minutes until golden and cooked through.
10. Serve warm, optionally with butter.

Nutritional Value (Amount per Serving):

Calories: 358; Fat: 10.46; Carb: 53.82; Protein: 11.67

Smoked Salmon and Cream Cheese Pinwheels

Prep Time: 15 Minutes   Cook Time: 10 Minutes   Serves: 4

Ingredients:

- 4 large flour tortillas
- 200g cream cheese, softened

- 200g smoked salmon slices
- 1/2 cucumber, thinly sliced
- 2 tablespoons chopped fresh dill
- Salt and pepper to taste

Directions:

1. Preheat Air Fryer to Bake at 180°C for 5 minutes and choose the MATCH option.
2. Spread cream cheese evenly over each tortilla.
3. Layer smoked salmon slices on top of the cream cheese.
4. Place cucumber slices on top of the smoked salmon and sprinkle with chopped fresh dill.
5. Season with salt and pepper to taste.
6. Roll up each tortilla tightly and slice into pinwheels.
7. Arrange pinwheels in a single layer in the preheated baskets.
8. Bake for 8-10 minutes until tortillas are slightly crisp and filling is warmed through.
9. Serve warm.

Nutritional Value (Amount per Serving):

Calories: 376; Fat: 21.15; Carb: 28.71; Protein: 18.35

Prawn and Avocado Bruschetta

Prep Time: 15 Minutes   Cook Time: 5 Minutes   Serves: 4

Ingredients:

- 1 baguette, sliced into rounds
- 200g cooked prawns
- 1 ripe avocado, diced
- 1 small red onion, finely chopped
- 1 tablespoon chopped fresh parsley
- 1 tablespoon olive oil
- 1 tablespoon lemon juice
- Salt and pepper to taste
- Lemon wedges, for serving

Directions:

1. Preheat Air Fryer to Bake at 180°C for 5 minutes and choose the MATCH option.
2. Brush baguette slices with olive oil and arrange them in a single layer in the preheated baskets.
3. Bake for 3-5 minutes until the baguette slices are toasted and golden brown.
4. In a bowl, combine cooked prawns, diced avocado, chopped red onion, chopped fresh parsley, olive oil, lemon juice, salt, and pepper.
5. Top each toasted baguette slice with the prawn and avocado mixture.
6. Serve immediately with lemon wedges on the side.

Nutritional Value (Amount per Serving):

Calories: 619; Fat: 32.55; Carb: 24.52; Protein: 57.39

Crispy Pork Belly Bites

Prep Time: 20 Minutes   Cook Time: 30 Minutes   Serves: 4

Ingredients:

- 500g pork belly, skin removed and cut into bite-sized pieces
- 2 tablespoons soy sauce
- 1 tablespoon honey
- 1 tablespoon olive oil
- 2 cloves garlic, minced
- 1 teaspoon Chinese five-spice powder
- Salt and pepper to taste
- Spring onions, thinly sliced for garnish

Directions:

1. Preheat Air Fryer to Roast at 200°C for 5 minutes and choose the MATCH option.
2. In a bowl, mix soy sauce, honey, olive oil, minced garlic, Chinese five-spice powder, salt, and pepper.
3. Add pork belly pieces to the bowl and toss until evenly coated.
4. Arrange pork belly pieces in a single layer in the preheated baskets.
5. Roast for 25-30 minutes until the pork belly is crispy and cooked through, shaking the baskets halfway through cooking.
6. Transfer crispy pork belly bites to a serving plate and garnish with thinly sliced spring onions.
7. Serve hot as a delicious appetizer or snack.

Nutritional Value (Amount per Serving):

Calories: 725; Fat: 71.12; Carb: 8.22; Protein: 12.68

Baked Camembert with Cranberry Sauce

Prep Time: 10 Minutes   Cook Time: 15 Minutes   Serves: 4

Ingredients:

- 1 whole Camembert cheese
- 2 tablespoons cranberry sauce
- 1 sprig fresh rosemary
- 1 clove garlic, thinly sliced
- Breadsticks or crusty bread, for serving

Directions:

1. Preheat Air Fryer to Bake at 180°C for 5 minutes and choose the MATCH option.

2. Remove any packaging from the Camembert cheese and place it back in its wooden box, or wrap it in foil if it doesn't have one.
3. Score the top of the Camembert cheese with a sharp knife and insert thinly sliced garlic slices and fresh rosemary sprig into the cuts.
4. Place the Camembert cheese in its box or wrapped in foil in the preheated baskets.
5. Bake for 12-15 minutes until the cheese is melted and gooey.
6. Remove the Camembert cheese from the baskets and place it on a serving plate.
7. Spoon cranberry sauce over the top of the melted cheese.
8. Serve immediately with breadsticks or crusty bread for dipping.

Nutritional Value (Amount per Serving):

Calories: 660; Fat: 24.71; Carb: 83.34; Protein: 24.17

Mini Pork and Apple Sausage Rolls

Prep Time: 20 Minutes   Cook Time: 15 Minutes   Serves: 4

Ingredients:

- 250g pork sausage meat
- 1 apple, grated
- 1/4 teaspoon ground sage
- 1/4 teaspoon ground nutmeg
- Salt and pepper to taste
- 1 sheet puff pastry, thawed
- 1 egg, beaten
- Sesame seeds, for sprinkling

Directions:

1. Preheat Air Fryer to Bake at 200°C for 5 minutes and choose the MATCH option.
2. In a bowl, mix pork sausage meat, grated apple, ground sage, ground nutmeg, salt, and pepper until well combined.
3. Roll out puff pastry on a lightly floured surface and cut it into strips.
4. Spoon the pork and apple mixture onto each strip of puff pastry and roll up to enclose the filling.
5. Place the mini sausage rolls seam-side down on a baking tray lined with parchment paper.
6. Brush the tops of the sausage rolls with beaten egg and sprinkle with sesame seeds.
7. Arrange sausage rolls in a single layer in the preheated baskets.
8. Bake for 12-15 minutes until the pastry is golden brown and cooked through.
9. Serve hot, optionally with tomato sauce for dipping.

Nutritional Value (Amount per Serving):

Calories: 934; Fat: 67.15; Carb: 60.57; Protein: 23.91

Crispy Corn and Jalapeño Fritters

Prep Time: 20 Minutes   Cook Time: 15 Minutes   Serves: 4

Ingredients:

- 2 cups (300g) sweetcorn kernels, drained
- 2 jalapeños, seeded and finely chopped
- 1/2 cup (60g) plain flour
- 1/4 cup (30g) cornmeal
- 1 teaspoon baking powder
- 1/2 teaspoon paprika
- 2 eggs, beaten
- 2 tablespoons milk
- Salt and pepper to taste
- Cooking spray

Directions:

1. Preheat Air Fryer to Air Fry at 200°C for 5 minutes and choose the MATCH option.
2. In a bowl, combine sweetcorn kernels, chopped jalapeños, plain flour, cornmeal, baking powder, paprika, beaten eggs, milk, salt, and pepper until well mixed.
3. Drop spoonfuls of the corn mixture into the preheated baskets, leaving space between each fritter.
4. Lightly spray the tops of the fritters with cooking spray.
5. Air fry for 12-15 minutes until the fritters are golden brown and crispy.
6. Serve hot, optionally with sour cream or salsa on the side.

Nutritional Value (Amount per Serving):

Calories: 393; Fat: 15.27; Carb: 35.02; Protein: 29.36

Welsh Rarebit Bites

Prep Time: 10 Minutes   Cook Time: 10 Minutes   Serves: 4

Ingredients:

- 4 slices of bread, crusts removed and cut into bite-sized squares
- 200g grated mature cheddar cheese
- 2 tablespoons butter
- 1 tablespoon plain flour
- 1 teaspoon mustard powder
- 1/4 cup (60ml) stout or ale
- 1 tablespoon Worcestershire sauce
- Salt and pepper to taste
- Chopped chives for garnish

Directions:

1. Preheat Air Fryer to Bake at 180°C for 5 minutes and choose the MATCH

option.

2. In a saucepan, melt butter over medium heat. Stir in plain flour and mustard powder to form a roux.
3. Gradually add stout or ale, stirring constantly until smooth and thickened.
4. Remove from heat and stir in grated cheddar cheese until melted and well combined.
5. Season with Worcestershire sauce, salt, and pepper.
6. Place bread squares on a baking tray lined with parchment paper.
7. Spoon a dollop of the cheese mixture onto each bread square.
8. Arrange the topped bread squares in a single layer in the preheated baskets.
9. Bake for 8-10 minutes until the cheese is bubbly and golden.
10. Garnish with chopped chives and serve hot.

Nutritional Value (Amount per Serving):

Calories: 241; Fat: 11.16; Carb: 28.32; Protein: 7.28

Mini Yorkshire Puddings with Beef and Horseradish

Prep Time: 15 Minutes   Cook Time: 20 Minutes   Serves: 4

Ingredients:

- 1 cup (120g) plain flour
- 1 cup (240ml) milk
- 2 eggs
- Salt and pepper to taste
- 200g thinly sliced roast beef
- 4 tablespoons horseradish sauce
- Fresh parsley for garnish

Directions:

1. Preheat Air Fryer to Bake at 200°C for 5 minutes and choose the MATCH option.
2. In a bowl, whisk together plain flour, milk, eggs, salt, and pepper until smooth.
3. Pour the batter into a jug for easier pouring.
4. Remove the preheated baskets and pour a small amount of batter into each compartment, filling them about halfway.
5. Return the basket to the air fryer and bake for 15-18 minutes until the Yorkshire puddings are puffed and golden.
6. Meanwhile, spread horseradish sauce on each slice of roast beef.
7. Once the Yorkshire puddings are done, remove them from the basket and top each one with a slice of beef.
8. Garnish with fresh parsley and serve warm.

Nutritional Value (Amount per Serving):

Calories: 407; Fat: 23.63; Carb: 29.55; Protein: 18.53

Crispy Bubble and Squeak Patties

Prep Time: 15 Minutes   Cook Time: 15 Minutes   Serves: 4

Ingredients:

- 2 cups (300g) mashed potatoes
- 1 cup (150g) cooked Brussels sprouts, mashed
- 1 cup (150g) cooked cabbage, mashed
- 1 onion, finely chopped
- 2 cloves garlic, minced
- 2 tablespoons plain flour
- 1 egg, beaten
- Salt and pepper to taste
- Cooking oil for frying

Directions:

1. Preheat Air Fryer to Air Fry at 200°C for 5 minutes and choose the MATCH option.
2. In a large bowl, mix together mashed potatoes, mashed Brussels sprouts, mashed cabbage, chopped onion, minced garlic, plain flour, beaten egg, salt, and pepper until well combined.
3. Form the mixture into small patties.
4. Lightly grease the preheated basket with cooking oil.
5. Arrange the patties in a single layer in the baskets.
6. Air fry for 12-15 minutes until the patties are golden and crispy, flipping halfway through cooking.
7. Serve hot with your favorite dipping sauce.

Nutritional Value (Amount per Serving):

Calories: 153; Fat: 3.93; Carb: 24.87; Protein: 6.1

Scotch Quail Eggs

Prep Time: 30 Minutes   Cook Time: 15 Minutes   Serves: 4

Ingredients:

- 8 quail eggs
- 200g sausage meat
- 50g breadcrumbs
- 1 tablespoon chopped fresh parsley
- 1/2 teaspoon dried thyme
- Salt and pepper to taste
- Flour for coating
- 1 egg, beaten
- Cooking oil for frying

Directions:

1. Preheat Air Fryer to Bake at 180°C for 5 minutes and choose the MATCH

option.

2. Boil quail eggs for 2-3 minutes, then transfer to cold water and peel.
3. In a bowl, mix sausage meat with breadcrumbs, chopped fresh parsley, dried thyme, salt, and pepper until well combined.
4. Divide the sausage mixture into 8 equal portions.
5. Flatten each portion and wrap around a peeled quail egg, ensuring it's evenly covered.
6. Roll each sausage-coated quail egg in flour, then dip in beaten egg, and coat with breadcrumbs.
7. Lightly grease the preheated basket with cooking oil.
8. Arrange scotch quail eggs in a single layer in the baskets.
9. Bake for 12-15 minutes until golden and cooked through.
10. Serve hot or cold as a delicious snack.

Nutritional Value (Amount per Serving):

Calories: 333; Fat: 14.99; Carb: 33.45; Protein: 17.78

Crispy Cauliflower Buffalo Wings

Prep Time: 20 Minutes   Cook Time: 20 Minutes   Serves: 4

Ingredients:

- 1 head cauliflower, cut into florets
- 1 cup (120g) plain flour
- 1 cup (240ml) milk
- 1 cup (120g) breadcrumbs
- 1 teaspoon garlic powder
- 1 teaspoon paprika
- Salt and pepper to taste
- 1/2 cup (120ml) buffalo sauce
- 2 tablespoons melted butter
- Ranch or blue cheese dressing for dipping

Directions:

1. Preheat Air Fryer to Air Fry at 200°C for 5 minutes and choose the MATCH option.
2. In a bowl, whisk together plain flour, milk, garlic powder, paprika, salt, and pepper until smooth.
3. In another bowl, mix breadcrumbs with salt and pepper.
4. Dip cauliflower florets into the flour mixture, then coat with breadcrumbs.
5. Arrange coated cauliflower florets in a single layer in the preheated baskets.
6. Air fry for 18-20 minutes until golden and crispy, flipping halfway through cooking.

7. In a small saucepan, heat buffalo sauce and melted butter until combined.
8. Toss crispy cauliflower wings in the buffalo sauce mixture until evenly coated.
9. Serve hot with ranch or blue cheese dressing for dipping.

Nutritional Value (Amount per Serving):

Calories: 323; Fat: 12.2; Carb: 46.91; Protein: 7.31

Crispy Black Pudding Croquettes

Prep Time: 20 Minutes   Cook Time: 15 Minutes   Serves: 4

Ingredients:

- 200g black pudding, casing removed and chopped
- 2 large potatoes, peeled and cubed
- 1 tablespoon butter
- Salt and pepper to taste
- 1 cup (120g) breadcrumbs
- 2 eggs, beaten
- Cooking oil for frying
- Optional: apple sauce for dipping

Directions:

1. Preheat Air Fryer to Max Crisp at 200°C for 5 minutes and choose the MATCH option.
2. Boil potatoes in salted water until tender, then drain and mash with butter until smooth. Season with salt and pepper.
3. In a pan, cook chopped black pudding over medium heat until crispy, then remove from heat and let it cool slightly.
4. Mix cooked black pudding with mashed potatoes until well combined.
5. Shape the mixture into small croquettes.
6. Dip each croquette into beaten eggs, then coat with breadcrumbs.
7. Lightly grease the preheated basket with cooking oil.
8. Arrange croquettes in a single layer in the baskets.
9. Max Crisp for 12-15 minutes until golden and crispy.
10. Serve hot, optionally with apple sauce for dipping.

Nutritional Value (Amount per Serving):

Calories: 296; Fat: 9.2; Carb: 44.94; Protein: 9.29

Smoked Mackerel Pâté with Melba Toast

Prep Time: 15 Minutes   Cook Time: 10 Minutes   Serves: 4

Ingredients:

- 200g smoked mackerel fillets, skin removed
- 100g cream cheese
- 2 tablespoons Greek yogurt
- 1 tablespoon lemon juice
- 1 tablespoon chopped fresh dill
- Salt and pepper to taste
- Melba toast or crackers for serving

Directions:

1. Preheat Air Fryer to Bake at 180°C for 5 minutes and choose the MATCH option.
2. In a food processor, combine smoked mackerel fillets, cream cheese, Greek yogurt, lemon juice, chopped fresh dill, salt, and pepper. Blend until smooth.
3. Transfer the mixture to a serving bowl.
4. Arrange melba toast or crackers in the preheated baskets.
5. Bake for 8-10 minutes until the toast is crispy and golden.
6. Serve the smoked mackerel pâté with warm melba toast or crackers.

Nutritional Value (Amount per Serving):

Calories: 208; Fat: 13.72; Carb: 4.58; Protein: 17.57

Welsh Cawl Spring Rolls

Prep Time: 30 Minutes   Cook Time: 20 Minutes   Serves: 4

Ingredients:

- 200g lamb shoulder, diced
- 1 onion, diced
- 1 carrot, diced
- 1 leek, sliced
- 1 tablespoon plain flour
- 500ml lamb or vegetable stock
- 200g potatoes, peeled and diced
- Salt and pepper to taste
- 8 spring roll wrappers
- Cooking oil for frying
- Mint sauce for dipping

Directions:

1. Preheat Air Fryer to Max Crisp at 200°C for 5 minutes and choose the MATCH option.
2. In a pan, brown diced lamb shoulder over medium heat until golden, then remove from the pan and set aside.
3. In the same pan, sauté diced onion, diced carrot, and sliced leek until softened.
4. Stir in plain flour and cook for 1-2 minutes.

5. Gradually add lamb or vegetable stock, stirring constantly until thickened.
6. Return the browned lamb shoulder to the pan, add diced potatoes, and season with salt and pepper.
7. Simmer for 20-25 minutes until the lamb is tender and the potatoes are cooked through.
8. Let the mixture cool slightly, then spoon it onto the center of each spring roll wrapper.
9. Fold the sides of the wrapper over the filling, then roll up tightly to enclose.
10. Lightly grease the preheated baskets with cooking oil.
11. Arrange spring rolls in a single layer in the baskets.
12. Max Crisp for 15-20 minutes until the spring rolls are golden and crispy.
13. Serve hot, optionally with mint sauce for dipping.

Nutritional Value (Amount per Serving):

Calories: 634; Fat: 24.4; Carb: 55.52; Protein: 46.15

Crispy Chicken Tenders with Honey Mustard Dip

Prep Time: 15 Minutes   Cook Time: 15 Minutes   Serves: 4

Ingredients:

- 1 lb (450g) chicken breast tenders
- 1 cup (120g) breadcrumbs
- 1/2 cup (60g) grated Parmesan cheese
- 1 teaspoon paprika
- 1/2 teaspoon garlic powder
- 1/2 teaspoon onion powder
- 2 eggs, beaten
- Cooking spray
- 1/4 cup (60ml) mayonnaise
- 2 tablespoons Dijon mustard
- 1 tablespoon honey
- 1 tablespoon lemon juice
- Salt and pepper to taste

Directions:

1. Preheat Air Fryer to Max Crisp at 200°C for 5 minutes and choose the MATCH option.
2. In a shallow dish, mix breadcrumbs, Parmesan cheese, paprika, garlic powder, onion powder, salt, and pepper.
3. Dip each chicken tender into the beaten eggs, then coat with the breadcrumb mixture, pressing gently to adhere.
4. Place the coated chicken tenders in a single layer in the preheated baskets.
5. Lightly spray the chicken tenders with cooking spray.
6. Max Crisp for 10-12 minutes, flipping halfway through, until the chicken is golden and cooked through.
7. While the chicken is cooking, in a small bowl, whisk together mayonnaise, Dijon mustard, honey, lemon juice, salt, and pepper to make the honey mustard dip.

8. Serve the crispy chicken tenders hot with the honey mustard dip on the side. Enjoy!

Nutritional Value (Amount per Serving):

Calories: 488; Fat: 28.1; Carb: 30.97; Protein: 28.47

Cheesy Veggie Stuffed Mushrooms

Prep Time: 20 Minutes   Cook Time: 15 Minutes   Serves: 4

Ingredients:

- 8 large mushrooms, stems removed and chopped
- 1 tablespoon olive oil
- 1 small onion, finely chopped
- 1 garlic clove, minced
- 1/2 red bell pepper, finely diced
- 1/2 green bell pepper, finely diced
- 1/2 cup (50g) grated cheddar cheese
- 2 tablespoons breadcrumbs
- Salt and pepper to taste
- Fresh parsley, chopped for garnish

Directions:

1. Preheat Air Fryer to Bake at 180°C for 5 minutes and choose the MATCH option.
2. In a pan, heat olive oil over medium heat. Add chopped mushroom stems, onion, garlic, and bell peppers. Cook until softened, about 5 minutes. Season with salt and pepper.
3. Stuff each mushroom cap with the cooked vegetable mixture.
4. Place stuffed mushrooms in the preheated baskets.
5. Bake for 10-12 minutes until mushrooms are tender and filling is heated through.
6. In a small bowl, mix grated cheddar cheese with breadcrumbs.
7. Sprinkle cheese mixture over the stuffed mushrooms and bake for an additional 3-5 minutes until cheese is melted and bubbly.
8. Serve hot, garnished with fresh parsley.

Nutritional Value (Amount per Serving):

Calories: 84; Fat: 4.83; Carb: 7.8; Protein: 4.23

Chapter 7: Desserts

Banoffee Pie

Prep Time: 20 Minutes   Cook Time: 15 Minutes   Serves: 4

Ingredients:

- 200g digestive biscuits
- 100g unsalted butter, melted
- 2 ripe bananas, sliced
- 100g dark chocolate, chopped
- 300ml double cream
- 1 tablespoon icing sugar
- Caramel sauce, for drizzling
- Chocolate shavings, for garnish (optional)

Directions:

1. Preheat the air fryer to bake at 160°C for 5 minutes and choose the MATCH option.
2. Place digestive biscuits in a food processor and pulse until finely crushed.
3. Transfer the crushed biscuits to a bowl and pour in the melted unsalted butter. Mix until well combined.
4. Press the biscuit mixture into the base and up the sides of greased pie dishes that fit in the baskets.
5. Bake the biscuit base in the preheated baskets for 10-12 minutes or until lightly golden. Remove and let it cool completely.
6. Once the base has cooled, arrange the sliced bananas over the bottom.
7. Sprinkle the chopped dark chocolate over the bananas.
8. In a separate bowl, whip the double cream and icing sugar until soft peaks form.
9. Spread the whipped cream over the chocolate layer.
10. Drizzle caramel sauce generously over the whipped cream.
11. Place the pie dishes back into the baskets.
12. Bake for 5 minutes or until the caramel sauce starts to bubble.
13. Once done, remove the pie from the baskets and let it cool slightly.
14. Chill the banoffee pie in the refrigerator for at least 2 hours or until set.
15. Before serving, garnish with chocolate shavings if desired.

Nutritional Value (Amount per Serving):

Calories: 667; Fat: 46.99; Carb: 55.32; Protein: 8.7

Blueberry Crisp

Prep Time: 15 Minutes   Cook Time: 30 Minutes   Serves: 4

Ingredients:

- 300g fresh blueberries
- 50g granulated sugar
- Zest of 1 lemon
- 1 tablespoon lemon juice

- 75g rolled oats
- 50g plain flour
- 50g unsalted butter, cold and cubed
- Vanilla ice cream, for serving

Directions:

1. Preheat the air fryer to roast at 180°C for 5 minutes and choose the MATCH option.
2. In a bowl, toss together fresh blueberries, granulated sugar, lemon zest, and lemon juice.
3. In another bowl, combine rolled oats, plain flour, and cubed unsalted butter. Rub the mixture between your fingertips until it resembles coarse crumbs.
4. Spread the blueberry mixture evenly in baking dishes that fit in the baskets.
5. Sprinkle the oat mixture over the blueberries.
6. Place the baking dishes in the preheated baskets.
7. Roast for 25-30 minutes or until the topping is golden and the blueberries are bubbling.
8. Once done, remove the crisp from the baskets and let it cool slightly.
9. Serve warm with a scoop of vanilla ice cream.

Nutritional Value (Amount per Serving):

Calories: 305; Fat: 9.15; Carb: 59; Protein: 6.24

Raspberry and White Chocolate Muffins

Prep Time: 15 Minutes   Cook Time: 20 Minutes   Serves: 4

Ingredients:

- 200g plain flour
- 100g granulated sugar
- 2 teaspoons baking powder
- 1/4 teaspoon salt
- 100g white chocolate, chopped
- 150g fresh raspberries
- 100ml milk
- 1 large egg
- 75g unsalted butter, melted
- 1 teaspoon vanilla extract

Directions:

1. Preheat the air fryer to bake at 180°C for 5 minutes and choose the MATCH option.
2. In a large bowl, mix together plain flour, granulated sugar, baking powder, and salt.
3. Stir in the chopped white chocolate and fresh raspberries.
4. In another bowl, whisk together milk, egg, melted unsalted butter, and vanilla extract.
5. Pour the wet ingredients into the dry ingredients and stir until just combined.

6. Divide the batter evenly among four greased muffin cups or silicone molds.
7. Place the muffin cups in the preheated baskets.
8. Bake for 18-20 minutes or until golden and a toothpick inserted into the center comes out clean.
9. Once done, remove the muffins from the baskets and let them cool slightly.
10. Serve warm or at room temperature.

Nutritional Value (Amount per Serving):

Calories: 558; Fat: 20.68; Carb: 84.93; Protein: 9.13

Sticky Ginger Pudding

Prep Time: 15 Minutes   Cook Time: 25 Minutes   Serves: 4

Ingredients:

- 150g pitted dates, chopped
- 150ml boiling water
- 1 teaspoon bicarbonate of soda
- 50g unsalted butter, softened
- 75g dark brown sugar
- 1 large egg
- 150g self-raising flour
- 1 teaspoon ground ginger
- 1/2 teaspoon ground cinnamon
- 1/4 teaspoon ground nutmeg
- Custard, for serving

Directions:

1. Preheat the air fryer to bake at 180°C for 5 minutes and choose the MATCH option.
2. In a heatproof bowl, pour boiling water over chopped dates and bicarbonate of soda. Let it sit for 10 minutes.
3. In another bowl, cream together softened butter and dark brown sugar until light and fluffy.
4. Beat in the egg until well combined. Stir in the soaked dates and any liquid.
5. Sift in self-raising flour, ground ginger, ground cinnamon, and ground nutmeg. Mix until just combined.
6. Divide the mixture evenly among four greased ramekins or silicone molds.
7. Place the ramekins in the baskets.
8. Bake for 20-25 minutes or until a skewer inserted into the center comes out clean.
9. Once done, remove the puddings from the baskets and let them cool slightly.
10. Serve warm with custard.

Nutritional Value (Amount per Serving):

Calories: 426; Fat: 9.13; Carb: 82.2; Protein: 6.9

Cherry Clafoutis

Prep Time: 15 Minutes   Cook Time: 25 Minutes   Serves: 4

Ingredients:

- 200g fresh cherries, pitted
- 50g granulated sugar
- 3 large eggs
- 100ml whole milk
- 50g plain flour
- 1 teaspoon vanilla extract
- Icing sugar, for dusting
- Whipped cream, for serving

Directions:

1. Preheat one basket to bake at 180°C for 5 minutes and choose the MATCH option.
2. In a bowl, toss together fresh cherries and granulated sugar.
3. In another bowl, whisk together eggs, whole milk, plain flour, and vanilla extract until smooth.
4. Grease pie dishes that fit in the baskets and arrange the cherries in the bottom.
5. Pour the egg mixture over the cherries.
6. Place the pie dish in the preheated baskets.
7. Bake for 20-25 minutes or until golden and set.
8. Once done, remove the clafoutis from the first basket and let it cool slightly.
9. Dust with icing sugar before serving.
10. Serve warm or at room temperature with whipped cream.

Nutritional Value (Amount per Serving):

Calories: 218; Fat: 5.35; Carb: 38.48; Protein: 4.43

Apple Turnovers

Prep Time: 20 Minutes   Cook Time: 15 Minutes   Serves: 4

Ingredients:

- 2 medium apples, peeled, cored, and diced
- 50g granulated sugar
- 1 teaspoon ground cinnamon
- 1/2 teaspoon ground nutmeg
- 1 tablespoon lemon juice
- 1 sheet ready-rolled puff pastry, thawed
- 1 egg, beaten
- Demerara sugar, for sprinkling
- Vanilla ice cream, for serving (optional)

Directions:

1. Preheat the air fryer to bake at 180°C for 5 minutes and choose the MATCH option.
2. In a bowl, combine diced apples, granulated sugar, ground cinnamon, ground nutmeg, and lemon juice. Mix well.
3. Roll out the puff pastry sheet and cut it into four equal squares.
4. Divide the apple mixture equally among the pastry squares, placing it in the center.
5. Fold the pastry over the filling to create triangles. Use a fork to crimp the edges to seal.
6. Brush the tops of the turnovers with beaten egg and sprinkle with demerara sugar.
7. Place the turnovers in the preheated baskets.
8. Bake for 12-15 minutes or until golden brown and crispy.
9. Once done, remove the turnovers from the baskets and let them cool slightly.
10. Serve warm, optionally with a scoop of vanilla ice cream.

Nutritional Value (Amount per Serving):

Calories: 792; Fat: 46.42; Carb: 84.92; Protein: 11.56

Lemon Cheesecake Bars

Prep Time: 20 Minutes   Cook Time: 25 Minutes   Serves: 4

Ingredients:

- 150g digestive biscuits
- 50g unsalted butter, melted
- 200g cream cheese, softened
- 50g granulated sugar
- Zest of 1 lemon
- 1 tablespoon lemon juice
- 1 large egg
- 50g sour cream
- 1 tablespoon plain flour
- Icing sugar, for dusting

Directions:

1. Preheat the air fryer to bake at 180°C for 5 minutes and choose the MATCH option.
2. Place digestive biscuits in a food processor and pulse until finely crushed.
3. Transfer the crushed biscuits to a bowl and pour in the melted unsalted butter. Mix until well combined.
4. Press the biscuit mixture into the base of greased baking dishes that fit in the baskets.
5. In a separate bowl, beat together cream cheese, granulated sugar, lemon zest, and lemon juice until smooth.
6. Add the egg, sour cream, and plain flour. Mix until well combined and

smooth.

7. Pour the cream cheese mixture over the biscuit base, spreading it evenly.
8. Place the baking dish in the preheated baskets.
9. Bake for 20-25 minutes or until set and lightly golden.
10. Once done, remove the baking dish from the baskets and let it cool slightly.
11. Dust with icing sugar before serving.
12. Serve chilled or at room temperature.

Nutritional Value (Amount per Serving):

Calories: 454; Fat: 27.83; Carb: 45.13; Protein: 7.66

Chocolate Chip Cookies

Prep Time: 15 Minutes   Cook Time: 10 Minutes   Serves: 4

Ingredients:

- 100g unsalted butter, softened
- 75g light brown sugar
- 50g granulated sugar
- 1 large egg
- 1 teaspoon vanilla extract
- 175g plain flour
- 1/2 teaspoon baking soda
- 1/4 teaspoon salt
- 100g chocolate chips

Directions:

1. Preheat the air fryer to bake at 180°C for 5 minutes and choose the MATCH option.
2. In a bowl, cream together softened unsalted butter, light brown sugar, and granulated sugar until light and fluffy.
3. Beat in the egg and vanilla extract until well combined.
4. In a separate bowl, sift together plain flour, baking soda, and salt.
5. Gradually add the dry ingredients to the wet ingredients, mixing until just combined.
6. Fold in the chocolate chips.
7. Scoop tablespoonfuls of dough and roll them into balls.
8. Place the cookie dough balls on greased baking sheets that fit in the baskets, leaving some space between them.
9. Place the baking sheets in the preheated baskets.
10. Bake for 8-10 minutes or until the cookies are golden brown around the edges.
11. Transfer the cookies to a wire rack to cool completely.

Nutritional Value (Amount per Serving):

Calories: 506; Fat: 22.5; Carb: 67.16; Protein: 8.06

Bread and Butter Pudding

Prep Time: 15 Minutes   Cook Time: 30 Minutes   Serves: 4

Ingredients:

- 6 slices white bread, crusts removed
- Butter, for spreading
- 50g sultanas
- 2 large eggs
- 300ml whole milk
- 50g granulated sugar
- 1 teaspoon vanilla extract
- Ground nutmeg, for sprinkling
- Custard, for serving

Directions:

1. Preheat the air fryer to bake at 180°C for 5 minutes and choose the MATCH option.
2. Spread butter on one side of each bread slice.
3. Cut the bread slices into triangles.
4. Arrange half of the bread triangles in a greased baking dish that fits in the basket, buttered side up.
5. Sprinkle half of the sultanas over the bread.
6. Repeat with the remaining bread triangles and sultanas.
7. In a bowl, whisk together eggs, whole milk, granulated sugar, and vanilla extract until well combined.
8. Pour the egg mixture over the bread and sultanas in the baking dishes.
9. Sprinkle ground nutmeg over the top.
10. Place the baking dishes in the preheated baskets.
11. Bake for 25-30 minutes or until golden and set.
12. Once done, remove the pudding from the baskets and let it cool slightly.
13. Serve warm with custard.

Nutritional Value (Amount per Serving):

Calories: 502; Fat: 20.03; Carb: 67.63; Protein: 12.15

Black Forest Cake

Prep Time: 30 Minutes   Cook Time: 25 Minutes   Serves: 4

Ingredients:

- 150g plain flour
- 50g cocoa powder
- 1 teaspoon baking powder
- 1/2 teaspoon baking soda
- 100g unsalted butter, softened
- 150g granulated sugar

- 2 large eggs
- 1 teaspoon vanilla extract
- 120ml buttermilk
- 100g pitted cherries, halved
- Whipped cream, for frosting and serving
- Chocolate shavings, for garnish (optional)

Directions:

1. Preheat the air fryer to bake at 180°C for 5 minutes and choose the MATCH option.
2. Grease and line the base of round cake tins that fits in the baskets.
3. In a bowl, sift together plain flour, cocoa powder, baking powder, and baking soda.
4. In another bowl, cream together softened unsalted butter and granulated sugar until light and fluffy.
5. Beat in the eggs, one at a time, until well combined.
6. Stir in vanilla extract.
7. Gradually add the dry ingredients to the wet ingredients, alternating with buttermilk, and mix until just combined.
8. Fold in the halved cherries.
9. Pour the batter into the prepared cake tin and spread it evenly.
10. Place the cake tins in the preheated baskets.
11. Bake for 20-25 minutes or until a skewer inserted into the center comes out clean.
12. Once done, remove the cake from the baskets and let it cool completely.
13. Frost the cake with whipped cream and garnish with chocolate shavings if desired.
14. Serve chilled or at room temperature.

Nutritional Value (Amount per Serving):

Calories: 551; Fat: 18.85; Carb: 86.43; Protein: 9.75

Baked Apples

Prep Time: 10 Minutes   Cook Time: 20 Minutes   Serves: 4

Ingredients:

- 4 apples, cored
- 50g brown sugar
- 1 teaspoon ground cinnamon
- 25g unsalted butter, softened
- 50g rolled oats
- 25g chopped nuts (such as walnuts or pecans)

- Vanilla ice cream, for serving

Directions:

1. Preheat the air fryer to roast at 180°C for 5 minutes and choose the MATCH option.
2. In a small bowl, mix brown sugar, ground cinnamon, softened unsalted butter, rolled oats, and chopped nuts until combined.
3. Stuff each cored apple with the oat mixture.
4. Place the stuffed apples in the preheated baskets.
5. Roast for 15-20 minutes or until the apples are tender.
6. Once done, remove the apples from the baskets and let them cool slightly.
7. Serve warm with a scoop of vanilla ice cream.

Nutritional Value (Amount per Serving):

Calories: 280; Fat: 9.45; Carb: 53.95; Protein: 4.49

Cinnamon Sugar Donut Holes

Prep Time: 15 Minutes   Cook Time: 10 Minutes   Serves: 4

Ingredients:

- 200g plain flour
- 50g granulated sugar
- 1 teaspoon baking powder
- 1/2 teaspoon ground cinnamon
- 1/4 teaspoon salt
- 100ml milk
- 1 large egg
- 50g unsalted butter, melted
- Vegetable oil, for frying
- 50g granulated sugar (for coating)
- 1 teaspoon ground cinnamon (for coating)

Directions:

1. Preheat the air fryer to max crisp at 180°C for 5 minutes and choose the MATCH option.
2. In a bowl, whisk together plain flour, granulated sugar, baking powder, ground cinnamon, and salt.
3. In another bowl, mix milk, egg, and melted unsalted butter until combined.
4. Gradually add the wet ingredients to the dry ingredients, stirring until just combined.
5. Roll the dough into small balls (about 1 tablespoon each).
6. Place the dough balls in the preheated baskets, ensuring they are not touching.

7. Max crisp fry for 5-7 minutes or until golden brown and cooked through.
8. While the donut holes are frying, mix granulated sugar and ground cinnamon in a shallow bowl.
9. Once done, remove the donut holes from the baskets and immediately roll them in the cinnamon sugar mixture until coated.
10. Serve warm.

Nutritional Value (Amount per Serving):

Calories: 375; Fat: 9.87; Carb: 65.17; Protein: 6.67

Coconut Macaroons

Prep Time: 10 Minutes   Cook Time: 15 Minutes   Serves: 4

Ingredients:

- 200g desiccated coconut
- 100g granulated sugar
- 2 large egg whites
- 1/2 teaspoon vanilla extract
- 50g dark chocolate, melted

Directions:

1. Preheat the air fryer to air fry at 160°C for 5 minutes and choose the MATCH option.
2. In a bowl, mix desiccated coconut and granulated sugar.
3. In another bowl, whisk egg whites and vanilla extract until frothy.
4. Gradually fold the egg white mixture into the coconut mixture until well combined.
5. Using a spoon or cookie scoop, shape the mixture into small mounds and place them on lined baking trays that fit in the baskets.
6. Air fry for 10-12 minutes or until the macaroons are golden brown.
7. Once done, remove the macaroons from the baskets and let them cool slightly.
8. Drizzle melted dark chocolate over the macaroons.
9. Let the chocolate set before serving.

Nutritional Value (Amount per Serving):

Calories: 192; Fat: 5.46; Carb: 32.72; Protein: 3.13

Peach Cobbler

Prep Time: 15 Minutes   Cook Time: 30 Minutes   Serves: 4

Ingredients:

- 4 ripe peaches, peeled and sliced
- 50g granulated sugar

- 1 tablespoon lemon juice
- 1/2 teaspoon ground cinnamon
- 75g plain flour
- 75g granulated sugar
- 1 teaspoon baking powder
- 1/4 teaspoon salt
- 60ml milk
- 50g unsalted butter, melted
- Vanilla ice cream, for serving

Directions:

1. Preheat air fryer to roast at 180°C for 5 minutes and choose the MATCH option.
2. In a bowl, combine sliced peaches, granulated sugar, lemon juice, and ground cinnamon. Mix well.
3. Transfer the peach mixture to greased baking dishes that fit in the baskets.
4. In another bowl, whisk together plain flour, granulated sugar, baking powder, salt, milk, and melted unsalted butter until smooth.
5. Pour the batter over the peach mixture.
6. Place the baking dishes in the preheated baskets.
7. Roast for 25-30 minutes or until the topping is golden and the peaches are bubbling.
8. Once done, remove the cobbler from the baskets and let it cool slightly.
9. Serve warm with a scoop of vanilla ice cream.

Nutritional Value (Amount per Serving):

Calories: 309; Fat: 7.92; Carb: 57.93; Protein: 3.69

Pumpkin Spice Bread

Prep Time: 15 Minutes   Cook Time: 35 Minutes   Serves: 4

Ingredients:

- 200g plain flour
- 1 teaspoon baking powder
- 1/2 teaspoon baking soda
- 1/2 teaspoon salt
- 1 teaspoon ground cinnamon
- 1/2 teaspoon ground ginger
- 1/4 teaspoon ground nutmeg
- 1/4 teaspoon ground cloves
- 100g granulated sugar
- 100g brown sugar
- 2 large eggs
- 150g canned pumpkin puree
- 80ml vegetable oil
- 60ml milk
- 1 teaspoon vanilla extract

Directions:

1. Preheat the air fryer to bake at 180°C for 5 minutes and choose the MATCH option.
2. In a bowl, sift together plain flour, baking powder, baking soda, salt, ground cinnamon, ground ginger, ground nutmeg, and ground cloves.
3. In another bowl, whisk together granulated sugar, brown sugar, eggs,

canned pumpkin puree, vegetable oil, milk, and vanilla extract until smooth.
4. Gradually add the dry ingredients to the wet ingredients, stirring until just combined.
5. Pour the batter into greased loaf pans that fit in the baskets.
6. Place the loaf pan in the preheated baskets.
7. Bake for 30-35 minutes or until a skewer inserted into the center comes out clean.
8. Once done, remove the bread from the baskets and let it cool slightly.
9. Slice and serve warm or at room temperature.

Nutritional Value (Amount per Serving):

Calories: 817; Fat: 42.91; Carb: 95.6; Protein: 18.61

Pear and Almond Tart

Prep Time: 20 Minutes   Cook Time: 25 Minutes   Serves: 4

Ingredients:

- 1 sheet ready-rolled puff pastry, thawed
- 2 ripe pears, thinly sliced
- 50g ground almonds
- 50g granulated sugar
- 1 large egg, beaten
- Flaked almonds, for garnish
- Icing sugar, for dusting

Directions:

1. Preheat the air fryer to bake at 180°C for 5 minutes and choose the MATCH option.
2. Roll out the puff pastry sheet on a lightly floured surface and transfer it to a baking sheets that fit in the baskets.
3. Sprinkle ground almonds evenly over the pastry, leaving a border around the edges.
4. Arrange the sliced pears on top of the ground almonds.
5. Fold the edges of the pastry over the pears, creating a rustic tart shape.
6. Brush the edges of the pastry with beaten egg and sprinkle flaked almonds over the top.
7. Place the tart in the preheated baskets.
8. Bake for 20-25 minutes or until the pastry is golden brown and crispy.
9. Once done, remove the tart from the first basket and let it cool slightly.
10. Dust with icing sugar before serving.
11. Serve warm or at room temperature.

Nutritional Value (Amount per Serving):

Calories: 1008; Fat: 69.86; Carb: 73.61; Protein: 23.35

APPENDIX RECIPE INDEX

Printed in Great Britain
by Amazon

38940760R00064